Game of Energy and Other Physi¿cs Puzzles

By Ian Roberts

Also, in the same series

Game of Genes and Other Biological Puzzles

Game of Elements and Other Chemical Puzzles

coming soon

Game of Stars and Other Astronomical Puzzles

Also, by the same author:

Aim for Grade 9: Astronomy

Aim for Grade 9: Radioactivity and Atomic Structure

Aim for Grade 9: Movement and Energy

WELCOME PUZZLERS!

As you are no doubt aware, solving all puzzles, whether found on-line or in books, employs a combination of one or more of the following skills: linguistic, pictorial, mathematical or logical (and possibly stretch to embrace the making of sociological and value judgements). The conundrums posed here also either use a physical situation or demand a basic understanding of PHYSICS.

Take for example Puzzle 1 which involves ideas of waves. Information has to be read, Physics and Maths understood to provide further information and logic applied to reach a solution of a LOGIC puzzle.

The popular SUDOKU puzzle has been amplified in Puzzle 19 so that understanding of Physics knowledge is needed, to obtain all the numbers required to solve it.

Other puzzles use varied combinations of skills within a Physics framework.

Answers usually include some explanation and the answer section is a large part of the book!

Some problems have a specific answer, others provide suggestions. A final one is enigmatic and will only be answered at a future date, maybe by YOU!

Good luck, but more importantly, ENJOY.

INDEX

1 WAVE LOGIC

The grid shows the speed and frequency of three waves A, B and C. Use the four statements to work out which wave has which speed, v, and which frequency,f.

$$v = f\lambda$$

		waves			speed (m/s)		
		A	B	C	10	100	1000
frequency (Hz)	1 000				✗	✗	✓
	10 000						✗
	100 000						✗
speed (m/s)	10						
	100						
	1 000						

Wave	f (Hz)	v (m/s)
A		
B		
C		

Information in clue 2 has also been entered in the grid.

1. Wave C is ultrasonic.
2. The wave of frequency 1000 Hz moves at 1000 m/s.
3. The wavelength of B is 1 m.
4. The wavelength of A is 1/1000 m.

2 SOME HISTORY OF SCIENCE

In the three lists below, Names and Contributions are in alphabetical order and the dates are in chronological order. But, the lists do not correspond horizontally.

Research to find links and arrange dates and contributions alongside names.

Name	Date	Contribution to humanity through Physics
Archimedes	250BC	discovered electrons
Bardeen	1610	discovered neutrons
Berners-Lee	1687	discovered law for the photoelectric effect
Chadwick	1897	discovered the nucleus
Einstein	1905	explained flotation
Galileo	1911	explained radiation from black holes
Hawking	1932	formulated the law of universal gravitation
Newton	1947	invented the Internet
Rutherford	1973	invented the transistor
Thomson	1989	showed phases of Venus

3 MOTION CROSSLINES

E
E
A
C
C
E

Clues are arranged in alphabetical order rather than their place in the grid. The shaded rectangle spells out a relevant word.

AN OBJECT WITH THIS TENDS TO STAY AT REST I _ _ _ _ _ _
FORCE WHICH MAKES AN OBJECT MOVE IN A CIRCLE C _ _ _ _ _ _ _ _ _ _
HAS ONLY SIZE (DIRECTION IS IMMATERIAL) S _ _ _ _ _
HAS SIZE AND DIRECTION V _ _ _ _ _
NOT MOVING S _ _ _ _ _ _ _ _ _
PRESSURE TIMES AREA F _ _ _ _
PROVIDES SPEED ON A DISTANCE-TIME GRAPH G _ _ _ _ _ _ _
REGULAR U _ _ _ _ _ _
RUTHERFORD'S PARTICULARLY MOVING FRIEND A _ _ _ _
SCALAR EQUIVALENT OF DISPLACEMENT D _ _ _ _ _ _ _
SCALAR EQUIVALENT OF VELOCITY S _ _ _ _
THIS IS INCLINED TO MAKE OBJECTS ROLL FASTER P _ _ _ _

4 ASTRONOMY CROSSWORD

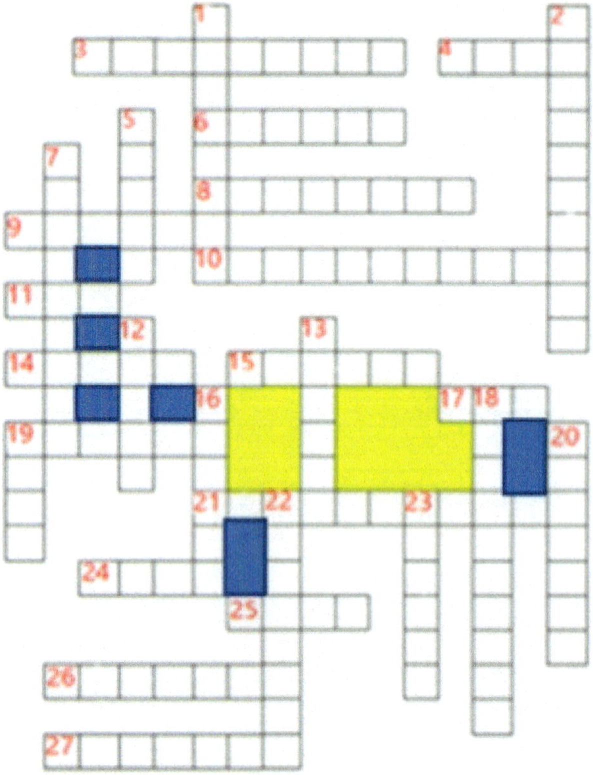

Across

3a strong stellar explosion
4a a nebula is this and gases
6a the Milky Way is one
8a Ceres is one
9a between Jupiter and Uranus
10a property giving stars colour
11a look up and see it
14a has a tail when near the Sun
15a emits flashes of light
17a number of stars in a binary
19a causes 'shooting stars'
21a end type of heavy stars
24a red planet
25a shape of an elipse
26a 'King' of the planets
27a most distant planet

Down

1d next stage for the Sun
2d absorbs U-V from stars
5d second planet from the Sun
7d end of some heavy stars
12d number of stars in Pleiades
13d orbit is nearly circular
16d 7th planet from Sun
18d Sirius-B is one
19d Ganymede is one
20d the fastest planet
22d everything
23d collapses forming a star

5 ANAGRAMS OF FAMOUS PHYSICISTS

Who are these people?

I charm seed	pare ` me
U.R.Ice	slice us
a far day	crocus pine
lava gin	gas us
site nine	hire the fan
a leg oil	eggier
fling me	red for hurt

I stew on a can

6 CROSSSUMS

(Give your answers to the number of sig.figs you can fit in the table.)

A3 across I when R = 3.00 kΩ and 66.0 V is across R.

A5 across Density of an object of m = 0.500 kg and v = 2.25 m^3.

B1 across The speed of an object which takes 20.0 s to travel 440 m.

A2 down The kinetic energy of a 1000 kg car moving at 2.0100 m/s.

C1 down λ for f = 0.014985 Hz and wave speed = 330.00 m/s.

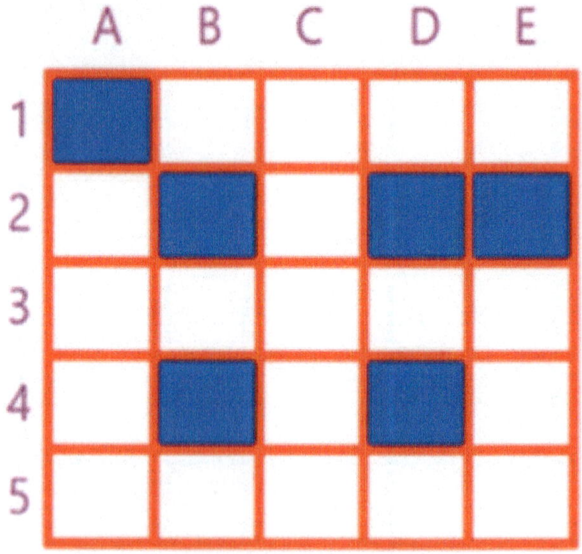
A
B
C
D
E
1
2
3
4
5

E3 down Momentum (in kg m/s) of a 0.73 kg moving at 0.304 km/s.

a **Which row(s) or column(s) in this table gives a number to two sig.figs?**

b **Place the numbers in the table in order of size, with the largest first.**

c **Place the numbers in order of the number of sig.figs. with the most first. (Use brackets if necessary to show equality of sig.figs.)**

7 PHYSCSDS = PHYSICS IDEAS 1 (WITHOUT VOWELS)

dnsty s mss / vlm

prssr qls frc vr r

frc s prprtnl t xtnsn

pwr s th rt f dng wrk

frc qls mss tms cclrtn

mmntm s mss tms vlcty

ngl f ncdnc qls ngl f rflctn

cclrtn qls th rt f chng f vlcty

wv spd qls frqncy tms wvlngth

wght qls mss tms grvttnl fld strngth

th spd f _ stllt cn b cnstnt bt th vlcty chngs

rd shft f glxs prvd vdnc tht th nvrs s xpndng

lllctrmgntcwvsrtrnsvrsndtrvltthsmspdnvcm

8 COG PICTURE

Three cogs are shown. When one cog is turned, its teeth force the teeth on the next cog to turn also.

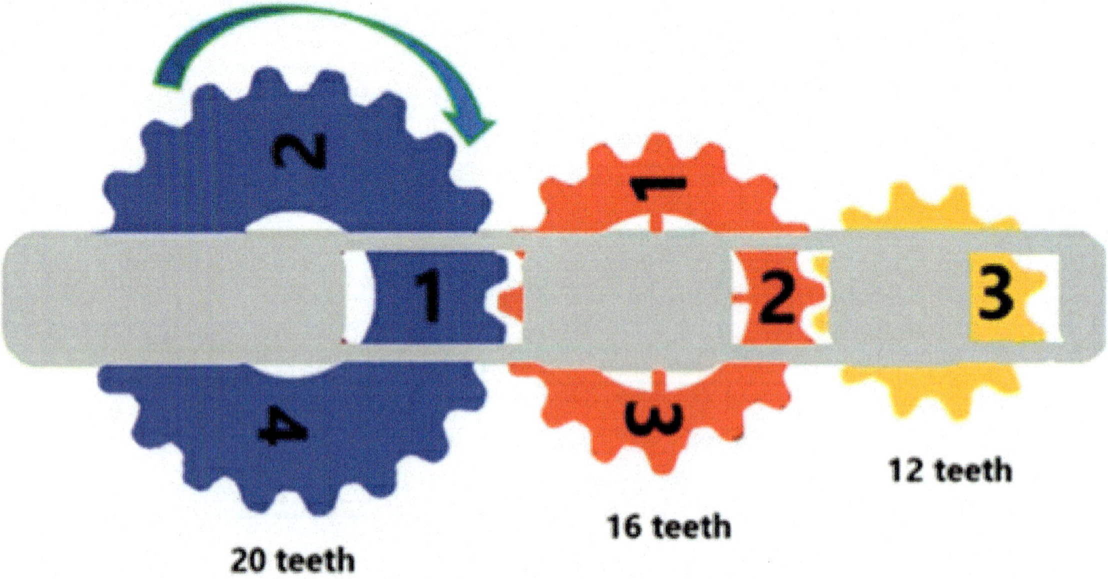

2
1
4
1
2
3
3
20 teeth
16 teeth
12 teeth

The number of teeth on each cog is also shown.
The number shown on the cogs, seen through the shaded screen, is 1 2 3.

a How many times will the 20 teeth cog have to rotate until the numbers again show up as 1 2 3?

b How many times must the 12 teeth cog turn to get 1 4 3 again?

9 IT TAKES TWO CROSSWORD

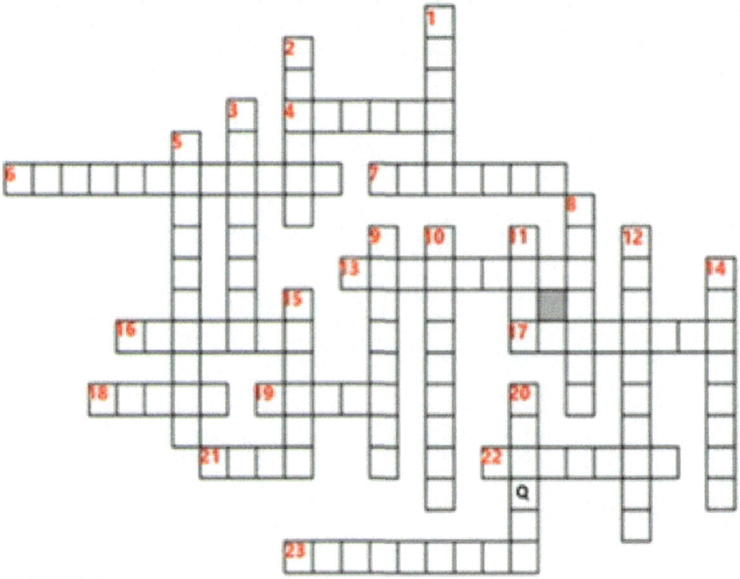

ACROSS

4 rocket's driving force
6 change of speed +/-
7 energy of motion
13 energy from position
16 'Iran tie' mixed up
17 final speed
18 velocity's scalar
19 turning point
21 slowing force
22 causes nebula's end
23 sense of moment

DOWN

1 famous as apple owner
2 paired with reaction
3 floating force
5 loved his bath
8 e.g. a hinge
9 F is its rate of change
10 overall effect
11 force caused by wings
12 g has no effect here
14 in equilibrium
15 competing
20 two equal forces causing rotation

10 RAINBOW

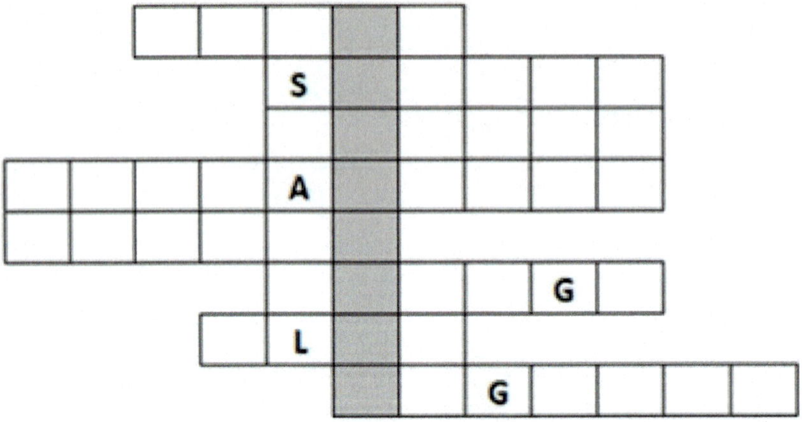
S
A
G
L
G

The answers to these clues will fit into the grid but are not in the correct order.

The shaded vertical rectangle will spell out a relevant word.

The process of changing the direction of light to cause this

Used in the laboratory to create this

A primary colour of light

A primary colour of paint and of light

The colour of the highest frequency

A complementary colour

A colour made by mixing two primary coloured paints

The different colours _ _ _ _ _ _ out to form this

11 DINGBATS 1

For Dingbats, you say what you see! E.g.

Horobod

stands for a famous outlaw dressed in Lincoln green

Robin Hood

The word 'rob' IN the word 'hood'.

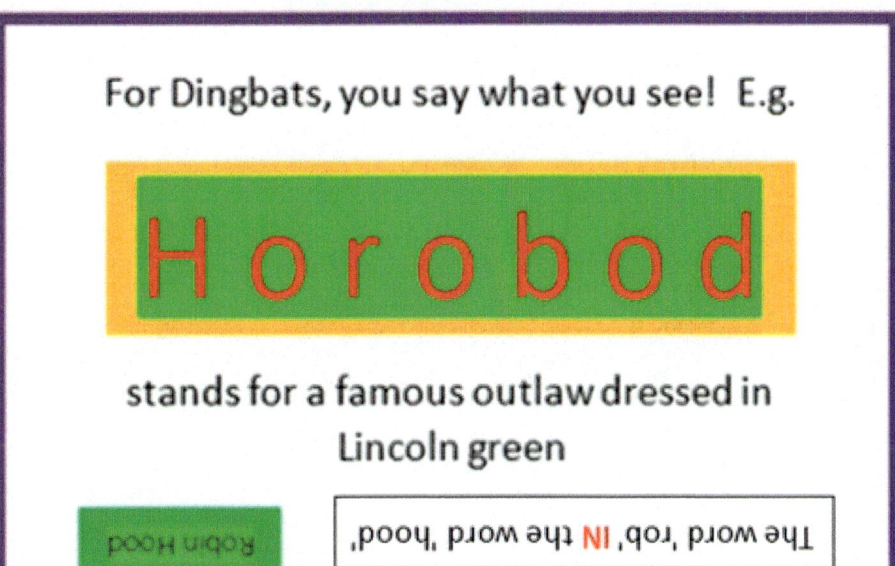

Now try these Physics ones

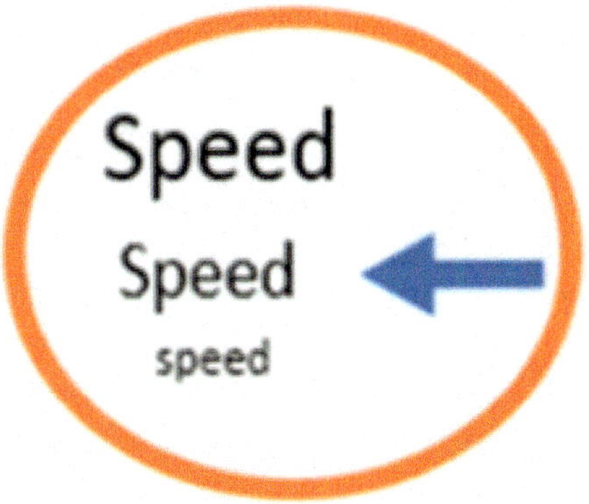
Speed
Speed
speed

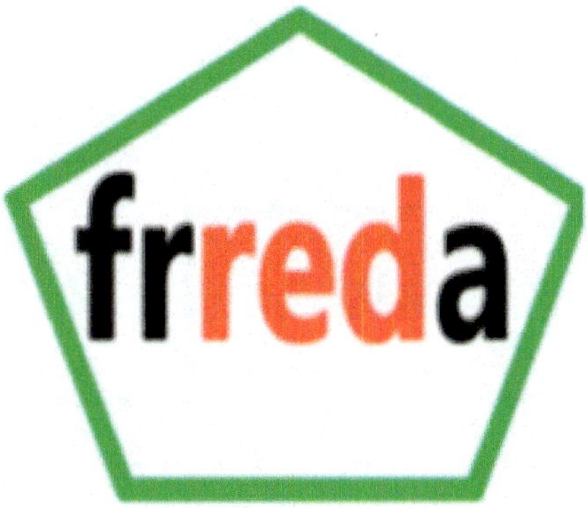
frreda

12 MORE DINGBATS

resistor

or RESISTOR

or rEsIsToR

DECAY

derefractivex

13 GOING ROUND THE MOON(S)

The diagram show the positions of two of Jupiter's moons, Ganymede and Europa, at various times in a month.

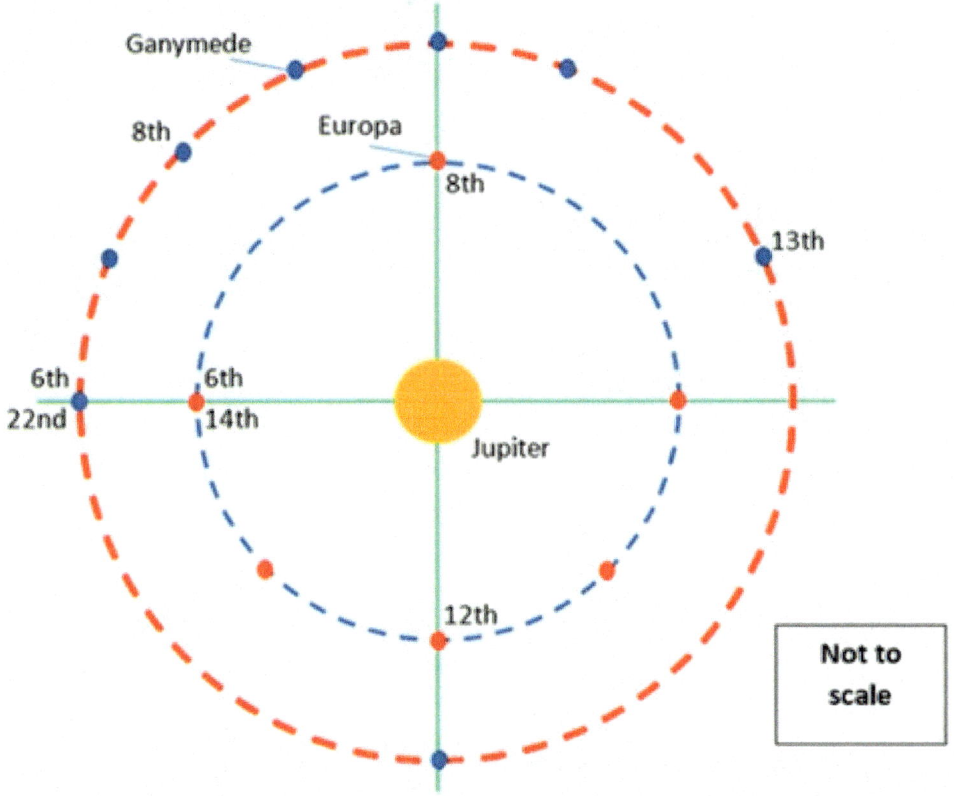
Ganymede
8th
Europa
8th
13th
6th
22nd
6th
14th
Jupiter
12th
Not to scale

The positions of the moons can be described in terms of the angle between them. The angles are those between the lines joining the moons to the centre of Jupiter. For example, the angle on the 8th of the month is 45°.

a **What is the angle on the 10th and on the 18th of the month?**

b **What is the appearance of a sketch graph of angle vs date?**

14 DENSE LOGIC

$d = m/v$

		mass/ kg				volume / $x\ 10^{-4}\ m^3$				density/ kg/m^3			
		0.64	1.40	2.10	5.44	2.0	4.0	5.0	8.0	800	2800	10500	13600
object	K												
	L												
	M												
	N												
density/ kg/m^3	800												
	2800												
	10500												
	13600												
volume / $x\ 10^{-4}\ m^3$	2.0												
	4.0												
	5.0												
	8.0												

1 K has a mass of 0.64 kg

2 L's volume is $4.0 \times 10^{-4}\ m^3$

3 M does not have the smallest volume

15 MEASURING VOLUME

Measuring volume with a calibrated jug or measuring cylinder is easy but more difficult using a container with no markings.

3 litres 4 litres

Imagine that you have only the two glasses shown above, a bowl and a sink to pour away any unwanted water.

One of the glasses holds exactly 3 litres (3l) and the other 4l.
You are asked to put different amounts of water into the bowl.
3l and 4l are very easy, as also are 6, 7, 8 and 9l.

ai How would you obtain 1l and 2l?

ii How many different ways can you obtain 7l?

b Can you obtain exactly 1 - 10l using pairs of glasses with volumes:
i (3l and 5l) and ii (4l and 7l)?

16 EARTHQUAKE CROSSWORD

ACROSS

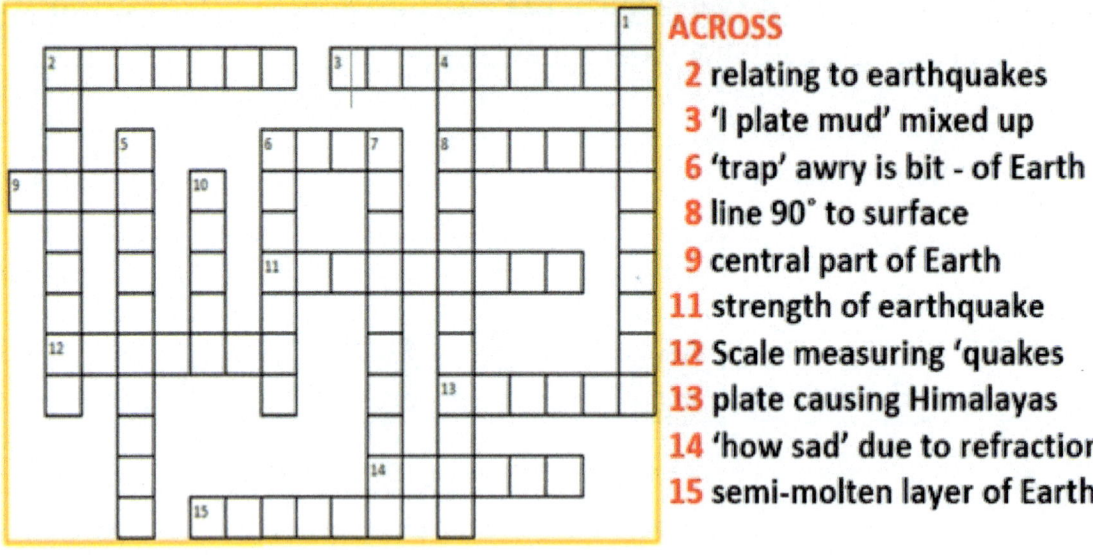

2 relating to earthquakes
3 'I plate mud' mixed up
6 'trap' awry is bit - of Earth
8 line 90˚ to surface
9 central part of Earth
11 strength of earthquake
12 Scale measuring 'quakes
13 plate causing Himalayas
14 'how sad' due to refraction
15 semi-molten layer of Earth

DOWN

1 process of changing direction in the same material
5 process of changing direction when speed changes
10 the outer layer of the Earth
2 transverse earthquake waves
4 vibration type of P-wave
6 type of wave arriving first
7 S-waves are this type of wave

17 UNITS WORDFIT

T
C
M

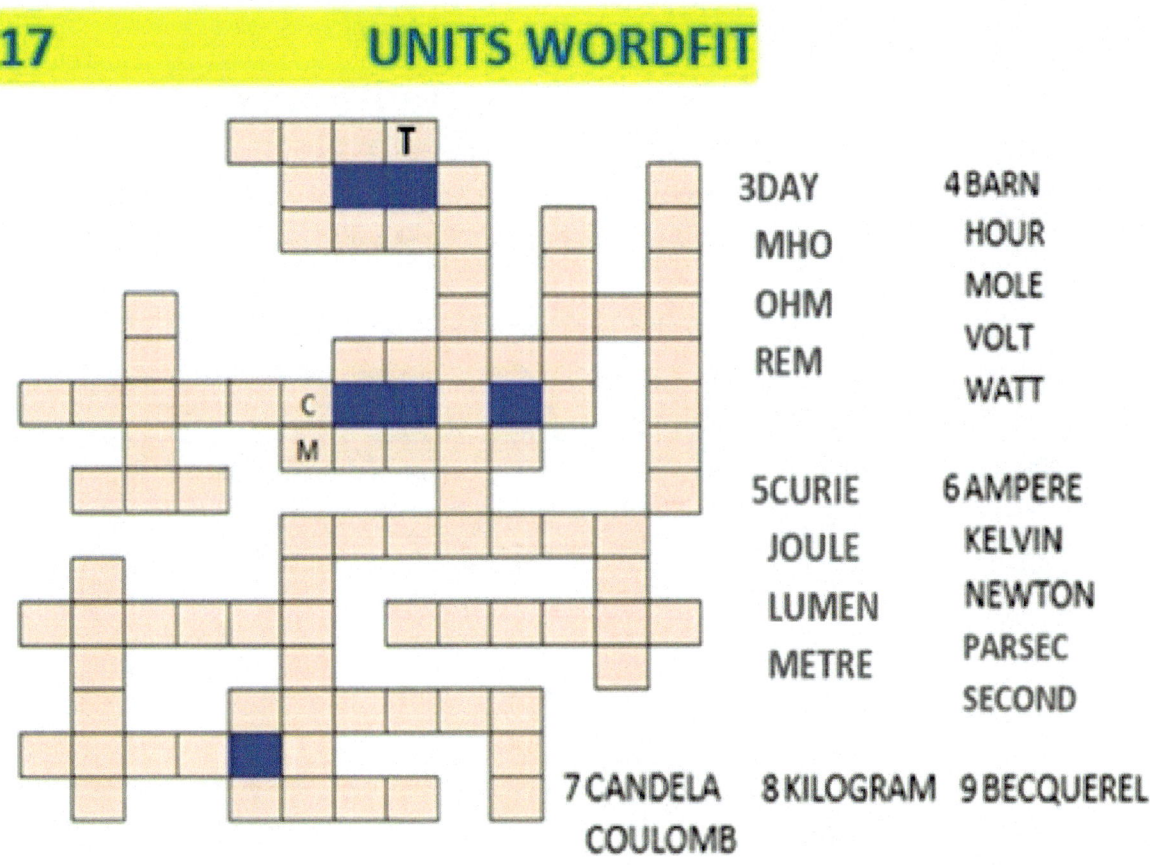

3 DAY
MHO
OHM
REM

4 BARN
HOUR
MOLE
VOLT
WATT

5 CURIE
JOULE
LUMEN
METRE

6 AMPERE
KELVIN
NEWTON
PARSEC
SECOND

7 CANDELA
COULOMB

8 KILOGRAM

9 BECQUEREL

[There may be three or four you do not know. What do they measure?]

18 ILLUMINATING WRITING

The way of writing words or titles can illustrate important facts or ideas relevant to the word while it is being written. Take, for example, Galileo. He is reputed to have compared speeds of fall of various objects of different mass from the Leaning tower of Pisa. We might convey these ideas like this:

Gali
e
o

One of the letters 'l' in his name is replaced by the tower and two letters/objects of different sized fonts are falling from it.

But Galileo was a polymath! So alternatively, we could write his name:

G a
i l e

a Explain why this is a good example of illuminating writing.

b Why are each of the following four examples quite good?

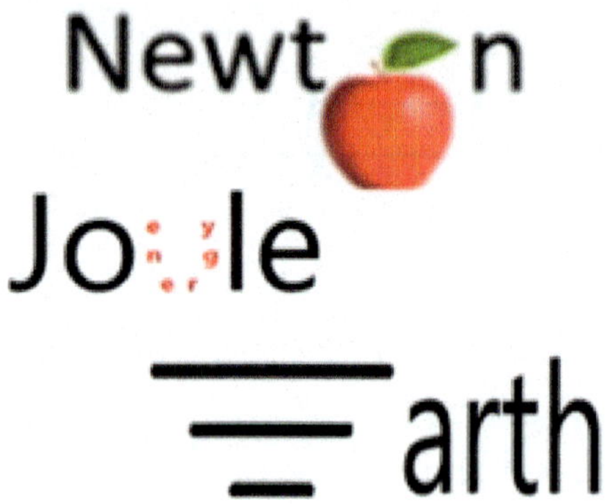
Newt n
Jo le
arth

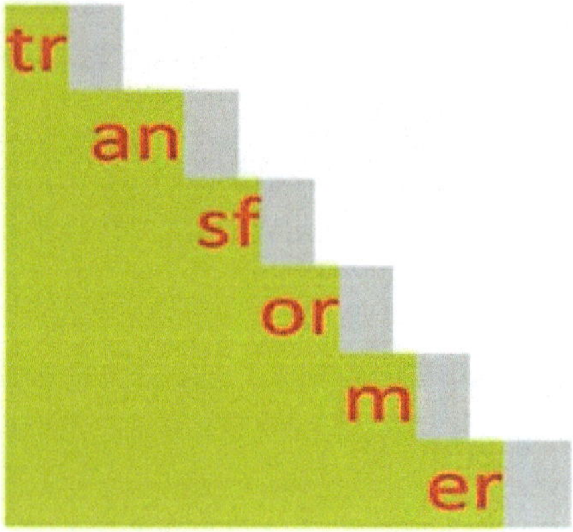
tr
an
sf
or
m
er

19 CLUEDOKU RADIOACTIVITY

Use the clues below to fill in some more numbers on the grid. Complete the grid by using the normal rules of Sudoku.

Each of the numbers 1-9 occurs just once in the answers.

[Suggestion: Check your answers before starting on the Sudoku!]

	A	B	C	D	E	F	G	H	I
1			3		6		8		
2				8			4		
3			6		2				
4					7			3	
5				1		5	6		
6		6						9	
7		8							
8			5		1	9			
9		7	9		8				

A7 no. of neutrons in a tritium (T) atom

C2 no. of n needed to initiate fission

D8 no. of nucleons in a molecule of HT

E5 no. of neutrons in an atom of 'O-17'

F2 no. of neutrons in a 'lithium 6' atom

G3 no. of electrons in a 'N-15' atom

G4 no. of p in nucleus after β-decay of a $^{7}_{4}Be$ nucleus

H7 no. of n and e in a 'lithium 6' atom

I6 no. of p in an 'oxygen 17' atom'

20 EARTHQUAKE LOGIC

This is about four randomly-chosen earthquakes

	YEAR 1934	YEAR 1988	YEAR 2004	YEAR 2005	DEATHS 3	DEATHS 8 000	DEATHS 86 700	DEATHS 250 000	MAGNITUDE 7.3	MAGNITUDE 7.6	MAGNITUDE 8.0	MAGNITUDE 9.2
KASHMIR												
MYANMAR												
NEPAL												
SUMATRA												
MAGNITUDE 7.3												
MAGNITUDE 7.6												
MAGNITUDE 8.0												
MAGNITUDE 9.2												
DEATHS 3	X	✔	X	X								
DEATHS 8 000		X										
DEATHS 86 700		X										
DEATHS 250 000		X										

Data for the first clue has been entered in the grid.

1 There were fewest fatalities in 1988
2 Most people died in Sumatra
3 The most recent quake was in Kashmir with an amplitude of 100 mm at 800 km
4 Fewer than 50 000 people died in 1934
5 The strongest earthquake was in 2004
6 The disaster giving an amplitude of 500 m at 680 km caused 8000 fatalities
7 The earliest tragedy was not in Myanmar

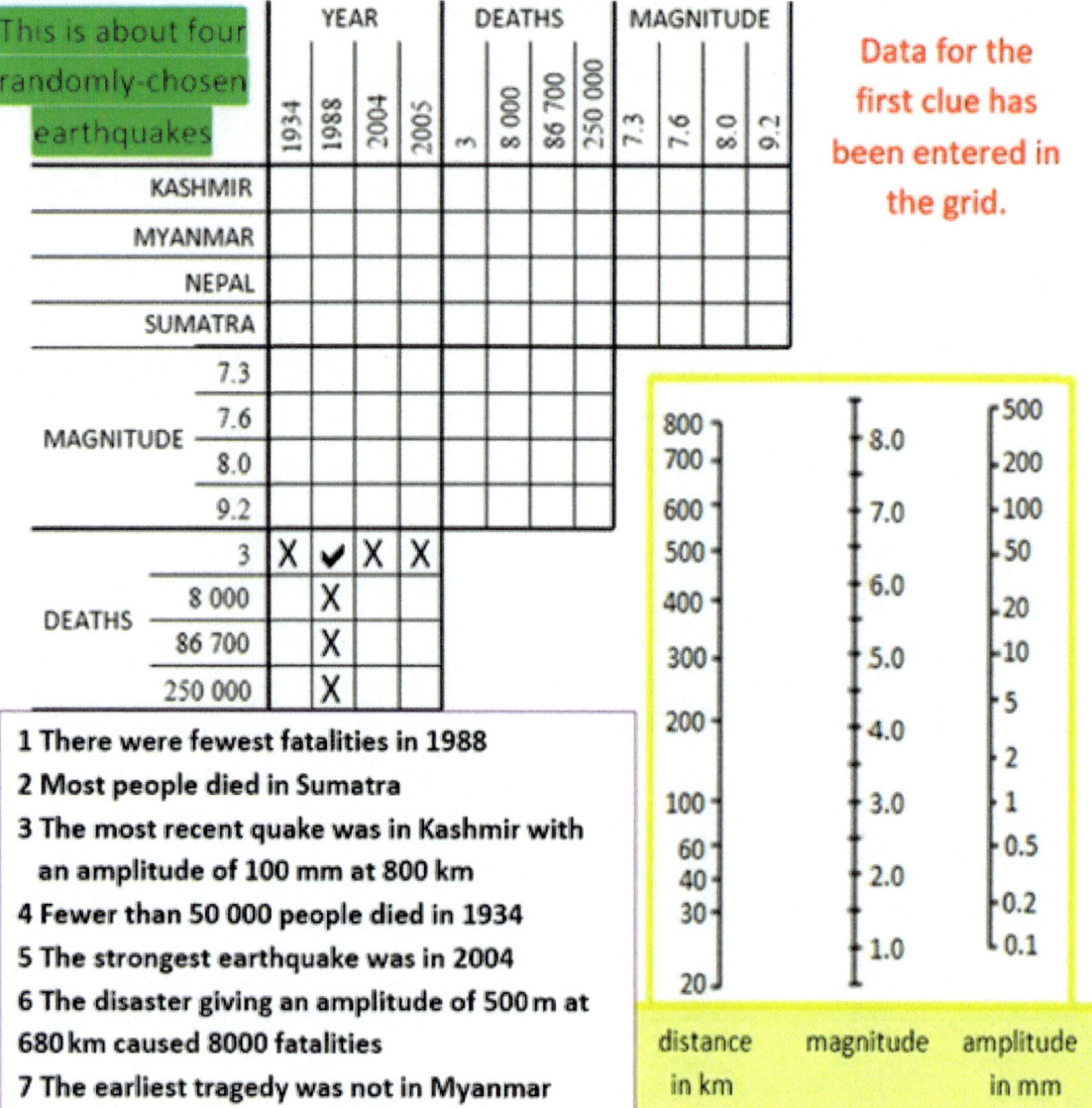

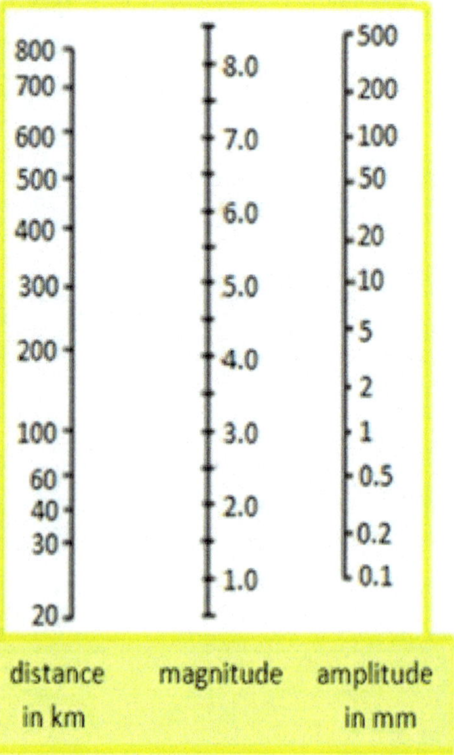
800
700
600
500
400
300
200
100
60
40
30
20
8.0
7.0
6.0
5.0
4.0
3.0
2.0
1.0
500
200
100
50
20
10
5
2
1
0.5
0.2
0.1
distance in km
magnitude
amplitude in mm

21 DINGBATS 2

MEXICAN
REFRACTION
CURRENT
tsurht
ice x ice x ice

22 MORE DINGBATS

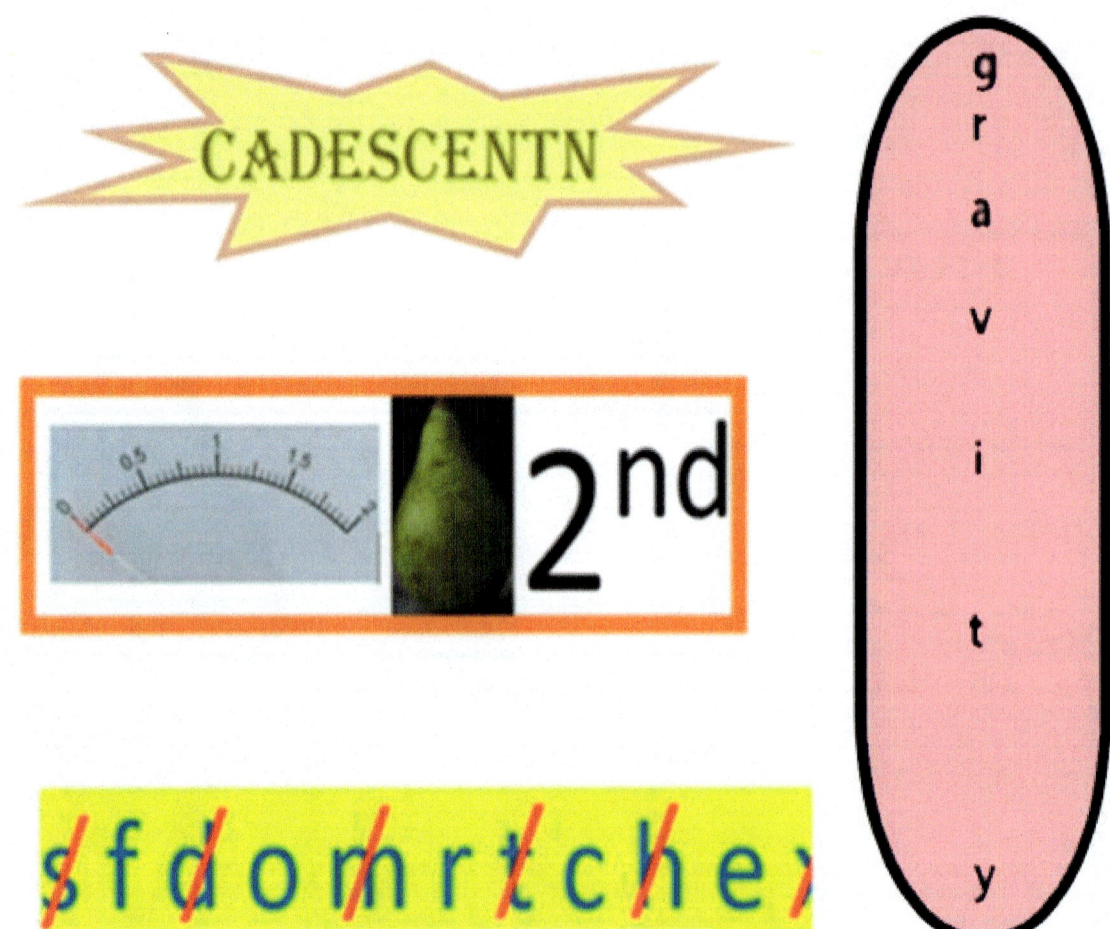

CADESCENTN

g
r
a
v
i
t
y

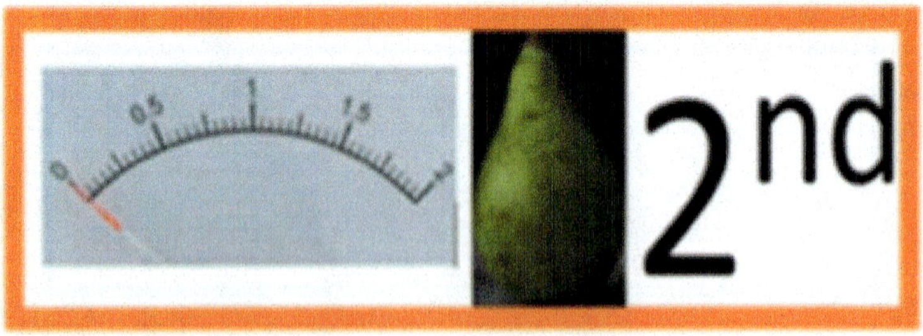
0
0.5
1
1.5
2
2nd

~~s~~f~~d~~o~~m~~r~~t~~c~~h~~e~~x~~

23 WAYS TO WEIGH

A protractor can be used to measure small masses. The weight holder can be made from graph paper according to the dimensions shown here. Attach it to one side of the protractor with cotton. Suspend the protractor from the edge of a bench with a plumb line in front. Balance the arrangement using modelling clay. The protractor should swing freely.

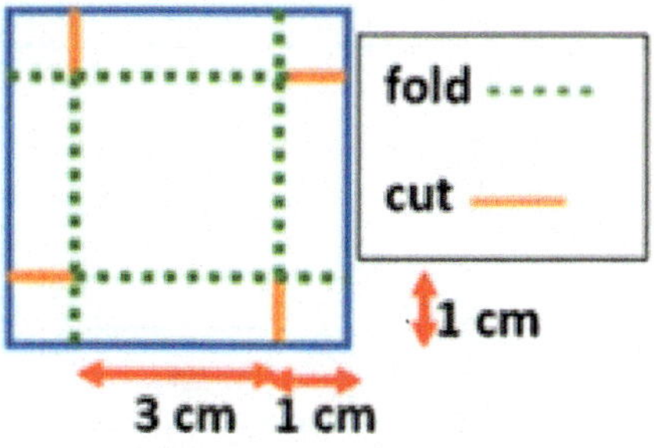
fold
cut
1 cm
3 cm
1 cm

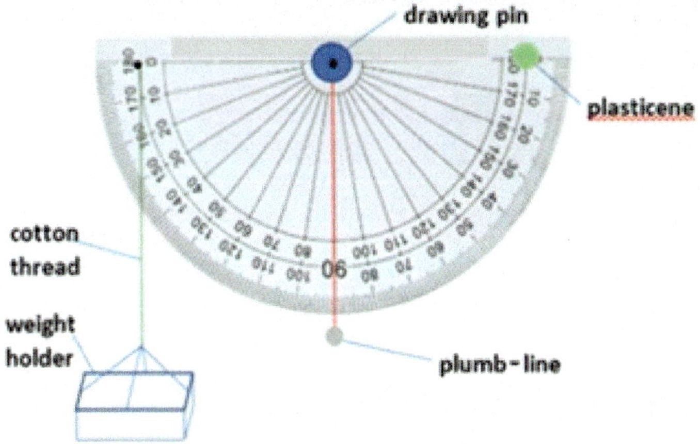
drawing pin
plasticene
cotton thread
weight holder
plumb-line

Cut some squares from graph paper to make equal 'weights. Add some paper weights to the weight holder noting the angle reading each time.

Draw a graph to calibrate the balance so as to measure mass by the angle turned.

a Can you find the mass of a small object e.g. a 1p coin.

b Can you explain the difference in care needed when measuring lengths to make the weight holder and the weights?

24 BALANCING WEIGHTS

The diagrams show arrangements of three weights on a balance.

The pivot is at the centre and you should ignore the plank's weight.

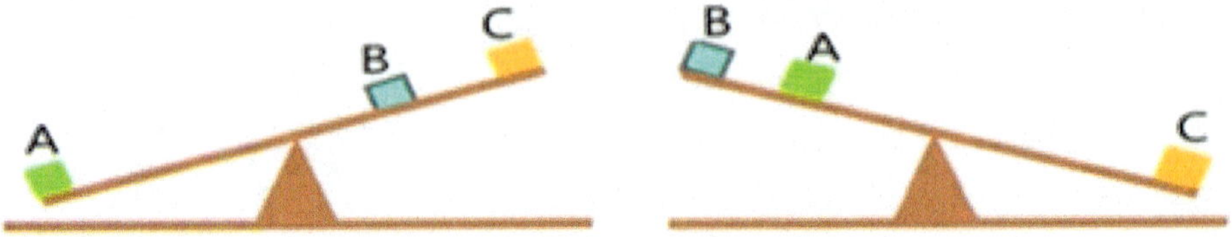
C
B
A
B
A
C

a Which of these six statements MUST BE correct?

A > B A > C B > A B > C C > A C > B

b In the next two diagrams, the arrangements are balanced and there are two weights at the ends and the third is half-way to the pivot.

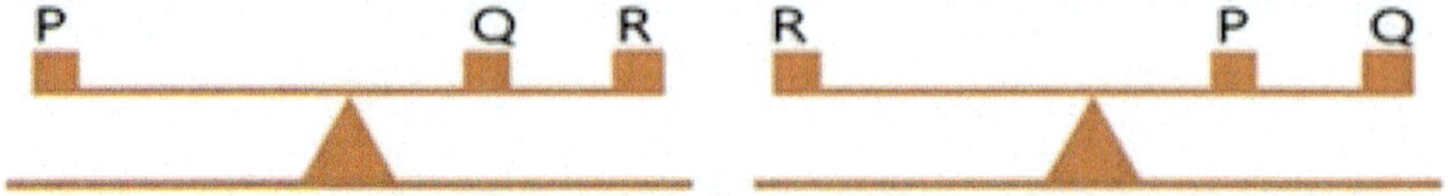
P
Q
R
R
P
Q

If Q = 6 units of weight, what are the weights of P and R?

25 VIEWING BABIES

Complete the chart by answering the clues.
The clues are in alphabetical order rather than the order in the grid.
The shaded vertical rectangle spells out a relevant word.

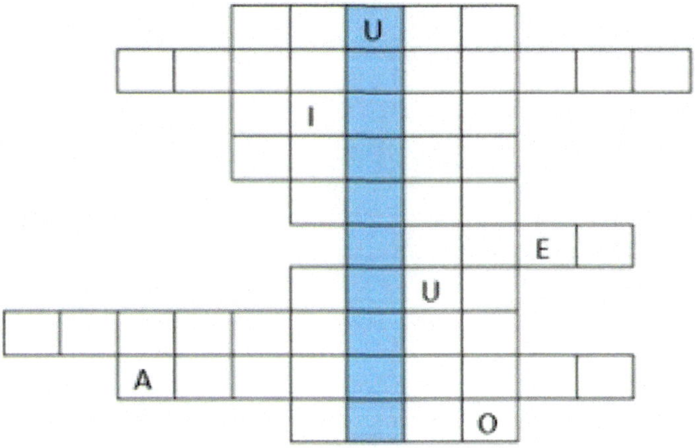
U
I
E
U
A
O

BETWEEN INFRA AND ULTRA AND AFTER EACH

DEFINITELY NOT QUIET

HEAR AGAIN

HIGH FREQUENCY, SOUNDS HIGH _ _ _ _ _

PERFORMED BY MEXICANS

RELATED TO INTENSITY

SCALAR OF VELOCITY

SPEED ÷ WAVELENGTH

SYMBOL IS GREEK LETTER FOR 'L'

UNIT OF FREQUENCY

26 FORCE AND MOTION WORDSEARCH

Find the given words in the grid. **Mind the spelling of the first word!!!**

A	A	C	V	B	E	T	N	I	E	R	O
A	C	E	L	L	E	R	A	T	I	O	N
C	C	O	E	V	C	N	A	E	O	N	E
C	E	C	D	E	R	C	D	E	R	O	R
T	L	V	E	L	O	C	I	T	Y	A	T
P	L	T	E	L	F	E	S	T	T	I	N
E	E	W	P	O	E	S	P	E	M	T	E
C	R	E	S	C	E	R	L	E	A	R	I
R	A	N	D	I	S	T	A	N	C	E	D
E	T	R	E	T	E	M	C	T	T	N	A
T	I	E	G	Y	A	D	E	V	I	I	R
N	O	F	R	A	V	I	M	T	O	O	G
I	N	O	I	T	C	A	E	R	N	A	N
A	H	R	R	N	E	D	N	O	C	E	S
M	D	C	A	L	D	M	T	O	C	F	E

ACCELERATION
ACTION
AEON
AREA
BEND
DAY
DEEP
DISPLACEMENT
DISTANCE
FORCE
GRADIENT
INERTIA

INTERCEPT LOCATE METER METRE RATE REACTION
ROOT SECOND SPEED TIME VELOCITY YEAR

27 FEELING HOT?

The diagram shows the parts of a mercury -in-glass thermometer.

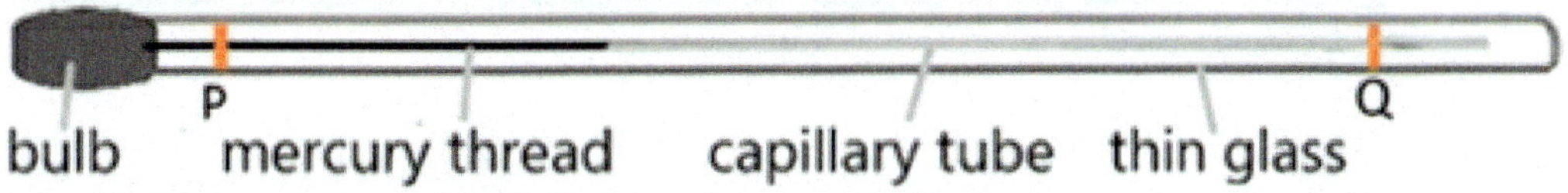
P
Q
bulb
mercury thread
capillary tube
thin glass

The bulb is placed at the test site and the mercury expands, moving the end of the thread along the capillary tube.

To make it useful, the position of the end of the mercury needs to be known at specific temperatures called the fixed points - 0°C and 100°C. The °C is for the Celsius scale but many other scales are possible and you may have heard of two: fahrenheit (°F) and kelvin (K).

°C
°F
100
212
0
32

a Research the values of the 'fixed points' (freezing and boiling points of water) on these two scales?

b In some cookery books, oven temperaturess are quoted in °F while the ovens are calibrated in °C. The chart alongside can be used to convert between these scales.

i Estimate the temperature in °F which corresponds to 60°C?

The equation for change is T°F = (T°C x 9/5) +32.

ii What temperature in °F corresponds to 60°C?

iii What is normal blood temperature (37.2°C) in °F?

28 OR HOTTER?

25°
19°

This thermometer was reputedly invented by Galileo. (Would temperatures obtained from it be measured in ˚G?)

The thermometer contains small, glass, hollow spheres of differing densities floating in a liquid (mostly water).

Each sphere has a labelled tag. The tag on the lowest floating sphere gives the temperature. The tag on the left shows the temperature to be about 19˚C.

As the temperature rises, the blue sphere sinks and the tag on the lowest floating sphere is 21˚.

Comment on the use of a Galilean thermometer in:

a the home

b scientific experiments

c hospitals.

[Anything which changes with temperature can be used (with varying successes and limitations) as a thermometer!]

29 RADIOACTIVITY CROSSWORD

ACROSS

4 escaped radioactive dust
8 force impeding fusion
10 the T in PET
12 useful energy from reactor
14 neutral parts of atom
18 nuclear equations balance mass and this
19 process when nuclei join
21 radioactivity discoverer
24 nuclei of same p different n
25 positive part of atomic nucleus
26 splitting of atoms

DOWN

1 treated by radiation
2 radiation from radon gas
3 nuclear fusion happens here
5 radiation effect on cells
6 particle used in smoke alarms
7 in time, the activity of a source ....
9 time for activity to halve
11 electromagnetic wave from nucleus
13 identity of beta particle
15 irregular nature of emission
16 double Nobel prize winner
17 lost during fusion
20 central part of atom
22 electron antiparticle
23 left when electron leaves

30 THERMAL LOGIC

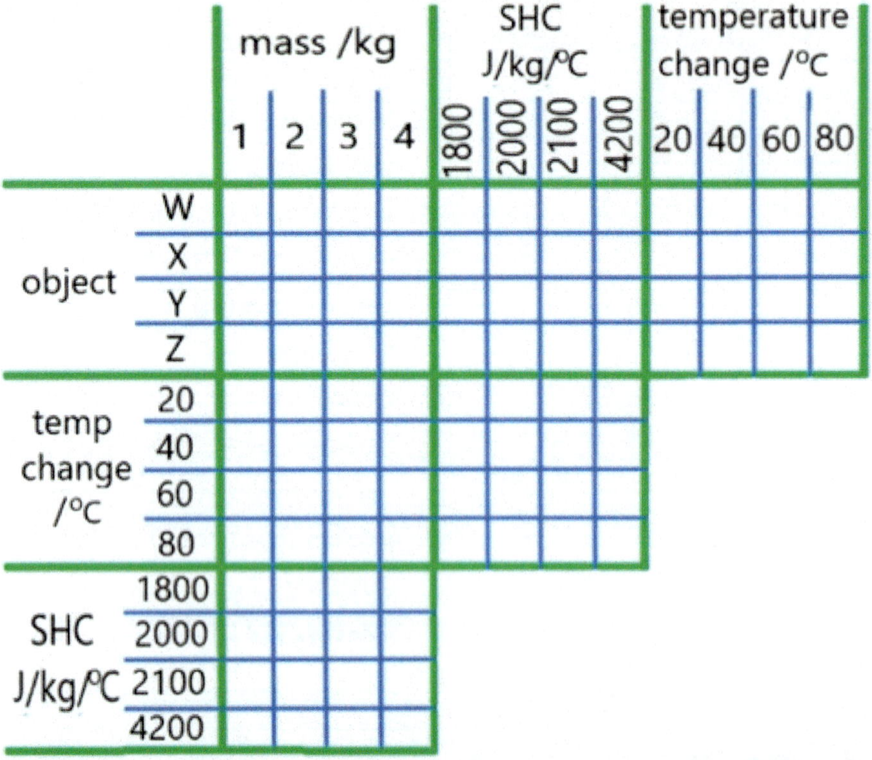
mass /kg
1
2
3
4
SHC J/kg/°C
1800
2000
2100
4200
temperature change /°C
20
40
60
80
object
W
X
Y
Z
temp change /°C
20
40
60
80
SHC J/kg/°C
1800
2000
2100
4200

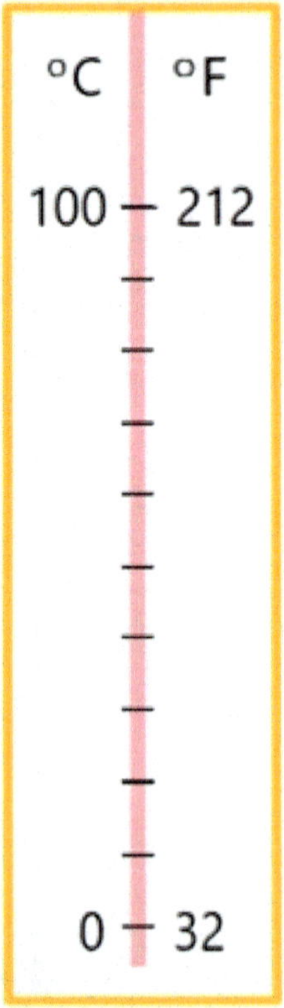
°C
°F
100
212
0
32

1. W's mass is 2 kg and changed temperature by 40°C when 168 000 J was provided.
2. The specific heat capacity (SHC) of Y is lower than X but higher than Z.
3. The smallest temperature change was for the object of SHC=4200 J/kg/°C.
4. The object of smallest mass changed temperature from 68°F to 212°F.
5. Object X is heaviest but does not have the greatest SHC.
6. Z did not have the greatest temperature change.

31 DINGBATS 3

l.f.

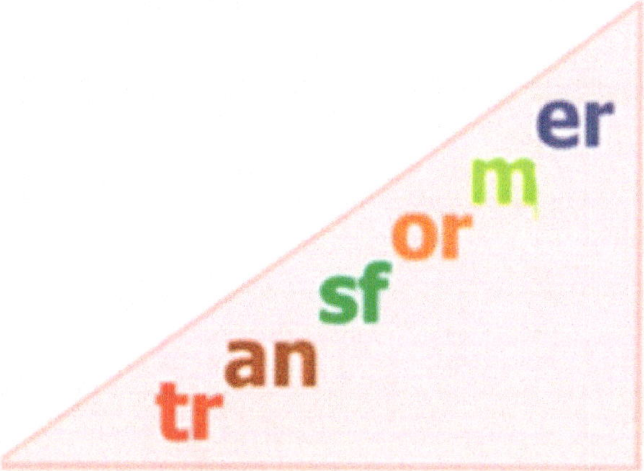
tr
an
sf
or
m
er

t h g i s

frsounda

32 RADIOACTIVE LOGIC

This grid refers to beams of alpha particles, protons, electrons and gamma rays.

		energy of beam in arbitrary units				charge number				mass number			
		5	10	15	20	+2	+1	0	-1	4	1	small	0
	A												
	B												
	C												
	D												
mass number	4												
	1												
	small												
	0												
charge number	+2												
	+1												
	0												
	-1												

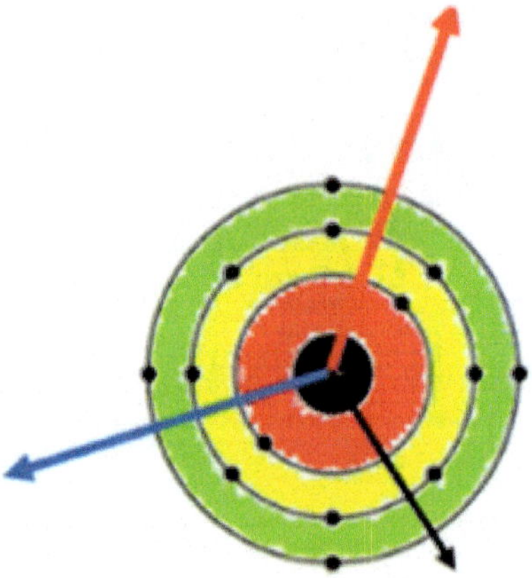

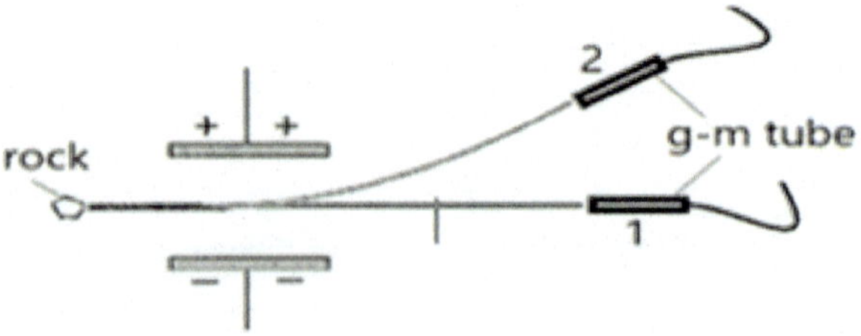
2
+ +
rock
g-m tube
1

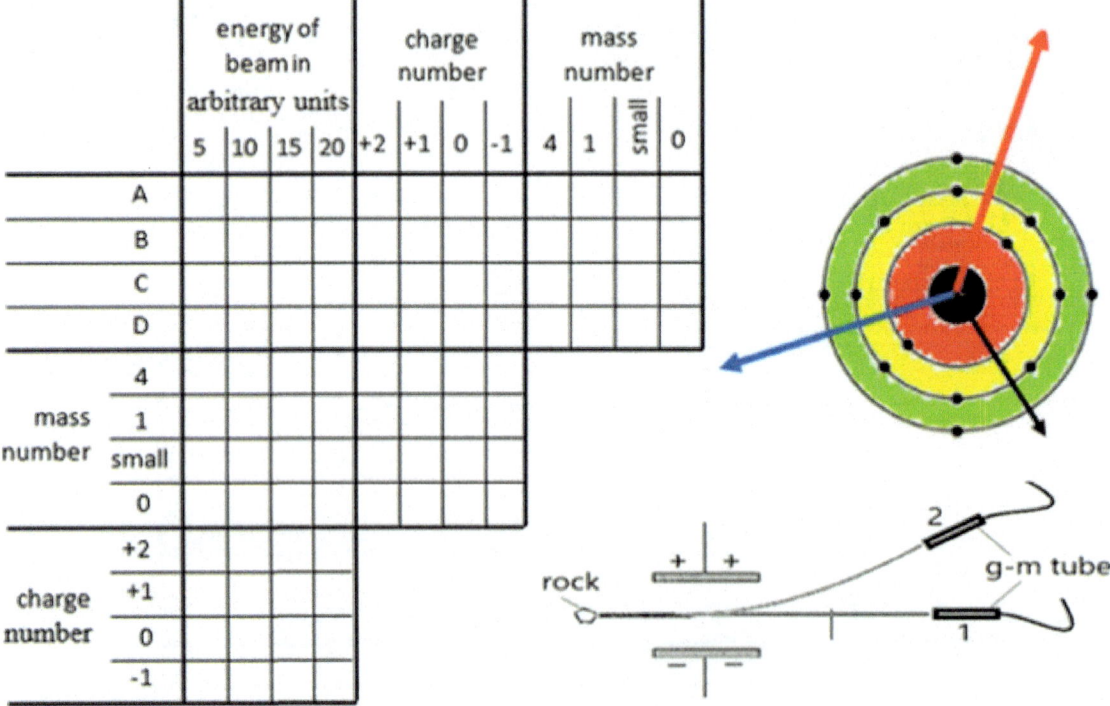

Use this information to identify A, B C and D.

1 **Particle B would be detected at position 2 in the diagram**

2 **C has an energy of 20 units but no mass**

3 **The particle which penetrates least has an energy of 5 units**

4 **A has 10 units of energy but is not an alpha particle**

33 Physcsds = PHYSICS IDEAS 2 (without vowels)

strss s prprtnl t strn .... (forces)

lkplsrplndnlkplsttrct .... (magnetism)

frcqlsrtfchngfmmntm .... (forces)

nrgytrnsfrrdqlschrgxptntldffrnc .... (current electricity)

hlflfsthtmtknfrhlfthndcydncltdcy .... (radioactivity)

wrkdnqlsfrcmltpldbydstncmvdndrctnffrc .... (forces)

wvstrnsfrnrgyndnfrmtnwthttrnsfrrngmttr .... (waves)

chngnthrmlnrgyqlsmssxspcfchtcpctyxchngntmprtr .... (matter)

frbdytbtcnstnttmprtrtndstrdtthsmvrgpwrthttbsrbs ... (conservation)

fssnfrnm235prdcstwdghtrnclndtwrmrntrnsplsrlsfnrgy.(radioactivity)

nrgycnntbcrtdrdstrydmrlychngdfrmnfrmtnthr .... (!!! always!!!)

34 ELECTROMAGNETIC WAVES

The clues to words for the grid are not in order.

The grey rectangle names a part of the electromagnetic spectrum

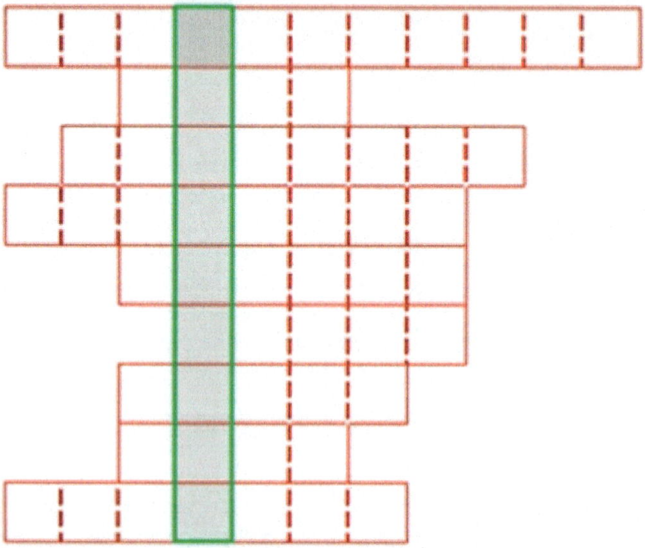

SEND A MESSAGE TO A FRIEND USING THESE WAVES C _ _ _ _ _ _ _ _ _ _

MATERIAL MOST AFFECTED BY THIS WAVE IN THE BODY W _ _ _ _

ALSO CALLED AN AERIAL A _ _ _ _ _ _

OPPOSITE OF WAVE EMITTER R _ _ _ _ _ _ _

WAVE WITH SLIGHTLY HIGHER FREQUENCY THAN THIS WAVE I _ _ _ _ _ _ _

WAVE WITH SLIGHTLY LONGER WAVELENGTH THAN THIS WAVE R _ _ _ _

USED TO RECEIVE SATELLITE TV WAVES D _ _ _

USED FOR COOKING WITH THESE WAVES O _ _ _

HAND-HELD INSTRUMENT TO COMMUNICATE VIA THESE WAVES M _ _ _ _ _

35 PHYSICS ANAGRAMS

halve Gwent
stag men
I put medal
sort trains
rain tie
vary at idiotic
Ron's tune
lace reaction
met no mum
squire fence
upstream tree
clasped in met
torn farmers
clip rate
no port
I race nests
their storm
I clean a quite bored tan coat into a purpose

36 ELECTRIC CROSSFIT

Complete the grid using words from the list.

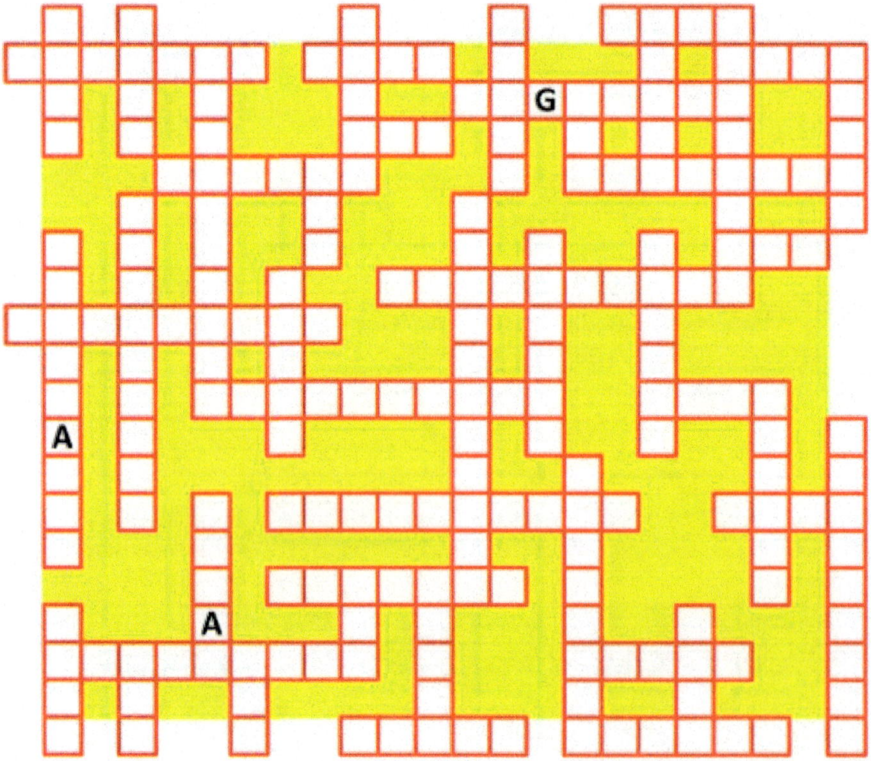
G
A
A

3
AMP
ARC
LDR
LED
OHM
RUB
SUN

4
ATOM
COIL
CORE
FUSE
IRON
LAMP
LIVE
VOLT
WATT

5
ANION
IONIC
JOULE
METAL
MOTOR
NOISE
POLES
STEEL
UNITS

6
AMPERE
DIRECT
ENERGY
MAGNET
STATIC

7
LATTICE
VOLTAGE

8
COULOMBS
ELECTRON
NEGATIVE
POSITIVE

9
CONDUCTOR
GENERATOR
INDUCTION
INSULATED
REPULSION

10
ATTRACTION
COMMUTATOR
RESISTANCE
THERMISTOR

11
ALTERNATING

37 COUNTING ROUND THE BEND

Follow the arrows round the bends to get from X to Y.

Do not move against an arrow.

Do not travel along the same line twice.

Count your score as you go along.

a What is the highest and the lowest score you can achieve?

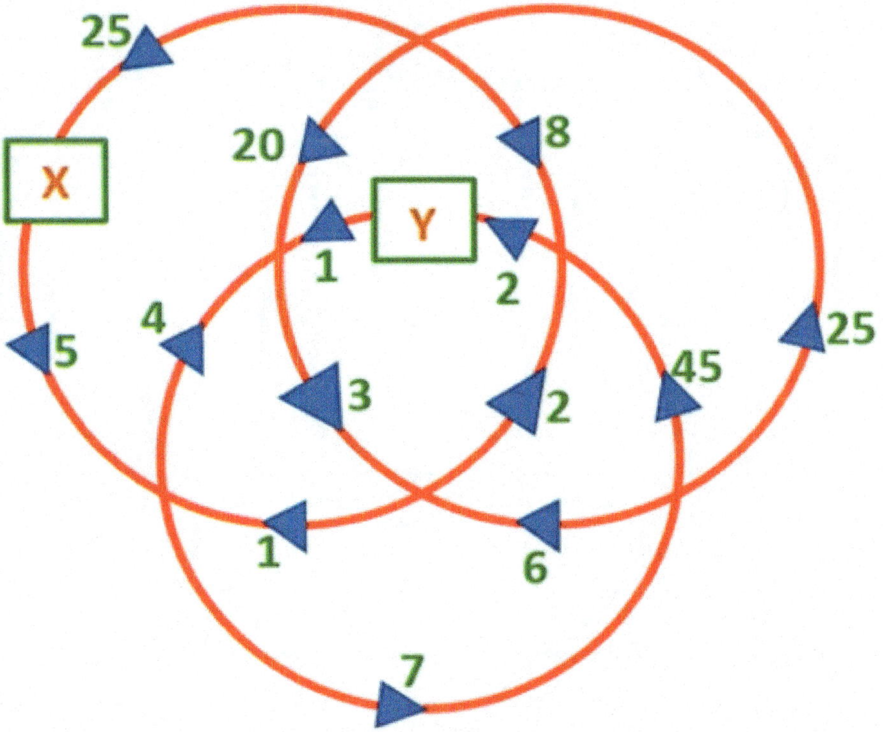

25
X
20
8
Y
1
2
4
5
25
45
3
2
1
6
7

b Which arrow, if reversed, will allow a score of 113?

38 MAKING A 'CUPPA' TEA

Some tea shops supply timers for brewing tea. They contain sand which can run slowly through a narrow hole when they are inverted.

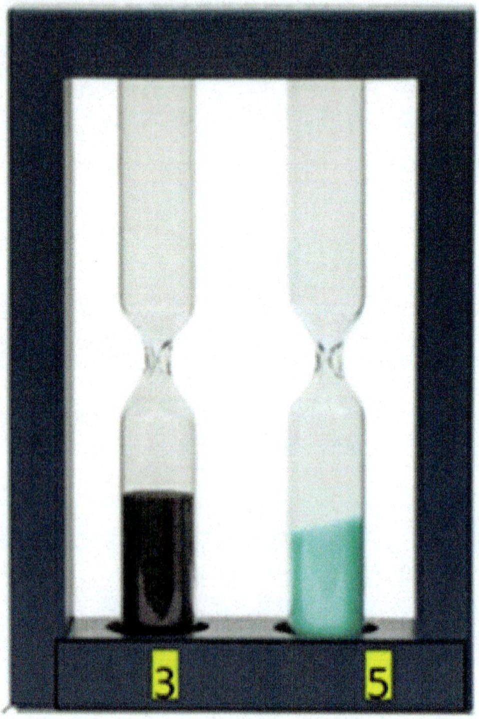
3
5

Imagine you have two timers - one for 3 mins and one for 5 mins.

a How can you arrange to measure
- 8 mins
- 6 mins
- 2 mins
- 1 min (after separating timers)

b If two separate timers were set for 3 mins and 4 mins, how could you arrange to time 1, 2 and 5 mins?

c If two separate timers were set for 4 mins and 5 mins, how could you arrange to time 2, 3 and 7 mins?

d Just a jiffy

You may have heard people referring to this as a small time interval. In astrophysics or in nuclear physics, it is in fact a very, very short interval – the time it takes light to travel a distance of 1 fermi (1×10^{-15} m) which is about equal to the diameter of a nucleon.

How many seconds are there in a jiffy?

39 CLUEDOKU RADIOACTIVITY

Complete the grid by first answering the clues and then using the techniques of Sudoku for the 9 categories of particles and processes.

Each of the numbers 1-9 is the answer to one clue only.

Advice: Check your answers to these before attempting the Sudoku.

	A	B	C	D	E	F	G	H	I
J	1				7				
K				5		1			
L		9						3	
M	6				3				4
N	8			6		4			5
O	7				2				3
P		3						6	
Q						9			
R					6				9

PROTON → 1
NEUTRON → 2
ELECTRON → 3
POSITRON → 4
ALPHA RAY → 5
BETA RAY → 6
GAMMA RAY → 7
FISSION → 8
FUSION → 9

AK negative part of an atom
CL used to measure thickness of Al
EK process which takes place in Sun
GP nuclear particle with no charge
HR radiation used to sterilise food

BJ antiparticle of an electron
DQ used in nuclear power plants
EQ Rutherford used one of these to explore inside atoms
IQ there are three of these in all lithium nuclei

40 FAMOUS PHYSICISTS CROSSWORD

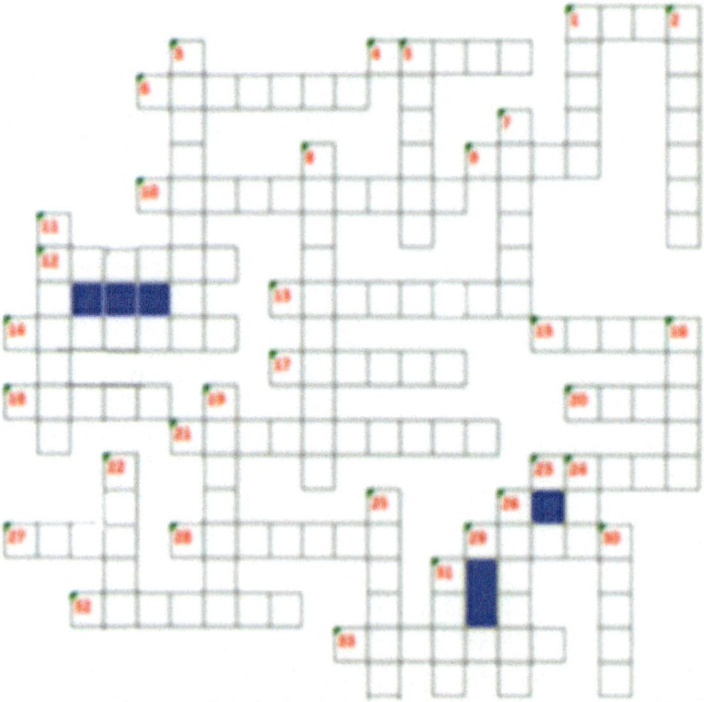

ACROSS

1 made discovery in 1879, first name Edwin

4+16down lady discovered Ra

6 unit of temperature

9 electromagnetism law 1834

10 discovered atomic nuclei

12 current measure

13 see 5 down

14 Rumford medal in 1860

15 shared Nobel prize 1933

17+30down discovered gravity

18 German, 1777 – 1855

20 Nobel prize 1922

21 outdated temperature scale

23 a very energetic man

27 made first practical phone

28 discovered Jupiter's moons

29 built first nuclear reactor

32author of 'A brief history of time'

33 discovered x-rays

DOWN

1 unit of frequency

2 Dutch 1902 Nobel prize winner

3 discovered radioactivity

5+13across -everything is relative

7 unit of temperature

8 Greek liked to keep clean

11 inventor of rubber balloon + +

16 see 4across

19 discovered animal electricity

22 Italian inventor of batteries

24 measurement of resistance

25 measures charge

26 a good counter

30 see 17across

31 a powerful man

41 'BODE'S' WELL FOR PLANETS

Neptune is a puzzling planet. A scientist, called Bode, devised this equation to predict the average orbital radius (α) for each planet in the Solar System.

$$\alpha = 0.4 + 0.3 \times 2^{m}$$

where m has the values: $-\infty$, 0, 1, 2, 3 .... (note: $2^{-\infty} = 0$, and $2^{0} = 1$)

a Complete the table to list the planets in order away from the Sun and then work out the values predicted by the equation. (Units based on Earth = 1)

planet	predicted orbital radius / units	actual orbital radius / units
		0.39
		0.72
Earth	1	1
Mars		1.52
Jupiter		5.20
		9.60
		19.2
Neptune		30.0

b Do the orbital radii of the four planets nearest the Sun fit the equation?

c Do the orbital radii of the next four planets (Jupiter to Neptune) fit?

d It has been suggested that the asteroid belt (between Mars and Jupiter) is the remains of a planet.

Does this suggestion help the fit?

BODE'S WELL CONTINUED

e **This chart includes data for the planets and for dwarf planet Ceres, in the asteroid belt, and for the dwarf planet Pluto.**

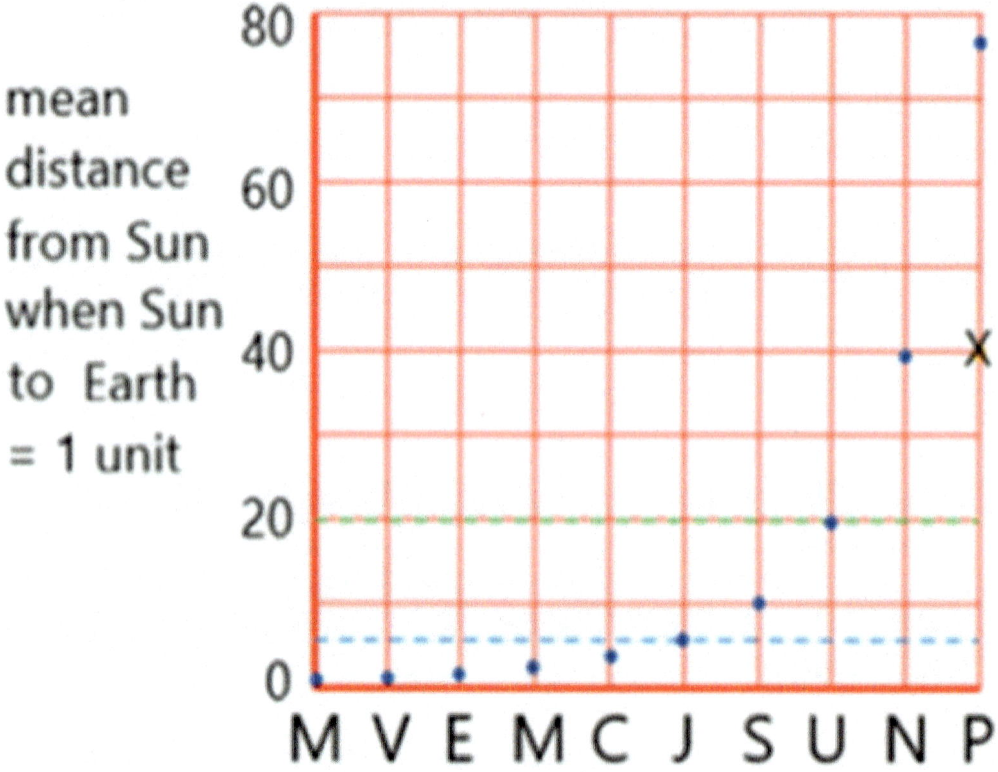
mean distance from Sun when Sun to Earth = 1 unit
80
60
40
20
0
X
M V E M C J S U N P

The cross plots the actual radius for Pluto's orbit.

Does the chart provide evidence for Neptune being an 'interloper' from outside our Solar System?

42 GUESSING OR ESTIMATING

Most people would have to guess if asked on which of the 6/7 continents a "Fossa" lives. (Some might look on the internet.) There is no reference point. Scientists often compare a value, in advance, with something about which they know. These scientific guesses or estimates need previous experience.

Are the following guesses or estimates?

a CURRENT - Four students looked at the brightness of a lamp carrying a current of 50 mA.
One student changed the current while the others had their eyes shut.
The other three students suggested values for the new current from the brightness of the bulb.
One suggested 41 mA, a second gave 43 mA and the third said 51 mA.
The three values were in error by 3 mA, 5 mA and 7 mA.
What was the actual current?

b DISTANCE - Three students, standing next to each other, proposed values for the separation of two distant trees which were being trimmed by woodsmen. One student gave 53 m, a second said 59 m and the third thought 54 m.
When they measured, the estimates were off target by 6 m, 7 m and 12 m.
What was the actual separation of the trees?

43 CURRENT AFFAIRS

This is part of a circuit for connecting to a battery across P and Q.

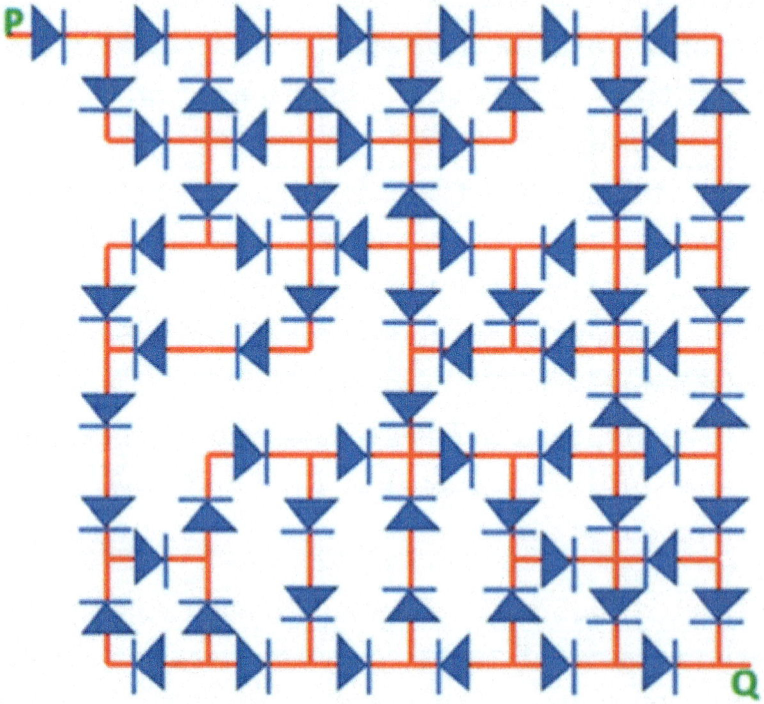
P
Q

It consists of many diodes which allow current only in the direction of the arrow.

Trace possible routes between P and Q and then produce a simplified circuit diagram which would have the same effect.

44 ESTIMATING/MEASURING

Measuring involves direct comparison against a fixed scale. But the units describing measurements are not always appropriate. For example, distances between atoms are in a totally different league to the distances separating stars. Scientists use various units for distances. One such unit is the light year (ly) – the distance light travels in one year.

a On average, Pluto is about 39 AU (astronomical units) from Earth, where one AU is equivalent to 1.5×10^{11} m.
What is the average separation of Earth and Pluto in ly?

b Astronomers also use the term 'parsec' (pc) for astronomical distances. 1 pc is 3.26 ly. Proxima Centauri, at 1.3 pc, is the nearest star to Earth.
How far from Earth, in AU, is Proxima Centauri?

c The prefix 'atto' (or a.....) stands for 10^{-18}. A distance of 1 attometre is roughly 1/1000 of the 'radius of a proton'!
Why might 1 apc (attoparsec) be considered a 'handy' size?

d Many length units are related to the human body.

i What factors affect the reproducibility of the measurement, for example, of a 'hand' as used to measure the height of a horse?

ii How many beard-seconds are there in 1 ly?
The beard second is a joke 'unit' suggested by some (male!) scientists. It is the amount the beard of a "standard scientist" (ha!) grows in 1 s!

[That's an awful lot of people standing chin to chin!]

45 RULES OF THE GAME– QUARKS (sub-atomic particles)

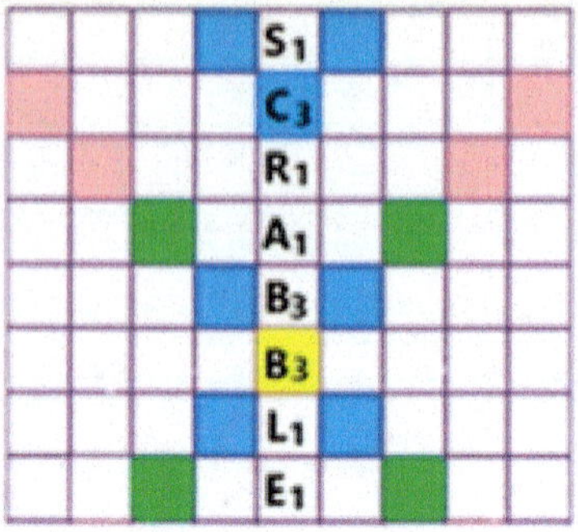
S1
C3
R1
A1
B3
B3
L1
E1

Like games, Physics has a set of rules. Thinking about quarks is an example. Some rules give possibilities while others restrict what is allowed.
Research the basic rules of Scrabble on line and we can imagine the start of this crossword-type game.
The first player chose the 7-allowed letters: E L B R Z B A and put the word R A B B L E on the board.
This word covers the yellow square, which under the rules doubles the score.

a How many points would this player score?

b Can you find a word with these letters that would score 52 instead of RABBLE?

The second player uses only 2 letters – S and C to extend the word shown.

c Show that this scores 17 points - remember the double letter score.

d The next player has the seven letters THERMAL.
How do you score 48 by adding 6 of these letters to one already on the board.

e What would you score if you put the same word in a different place?

f Research how many of each letter are available in the set.
Why do the rules NOT allow a player NOW to pick the 7 letters: B W T P L A N?

So, you have seen how to apply rules. What are the RULES FOR QUARKS?

- Inside each proton and each neutron, there are THREE quarks.
- These quarks are of ONLY TWO types called UP and DOWN.
- All UP quarks have the same charge.
- All DOWN quarks have the same charge (but different to that on UP quarks).

g Suggest values of charges on the three quarks (of the UP and the DOWN types) which could account for the +1 charge on a proton and 0 charge on a neutron?

[NOTE: The i-Game of Quarks will be extended in Puzzle 56!]

46 CLUEDOKU PROCESSES

Complete the grid by first answering the clues and then using the techniques of Sudoku for the 9 processes. The nine clues all have an answer which is a different one of the numbers 1-9.

	A	B	C	D	E	F	G	H	I
1						3			
2							3		
3				1					
4	5				7	6			4
5									5
6				2			1		
7			9						
8	8								
9	4			7	5				

CONDENSATION → 1
CONDUCTION → 2
CONVECTION → 3
EVAPORATION → 4
FISSION → 5
FUSION → 6
RADIATION → 7
REFLECTION → 8
REFRACTION → 9

A3 joining
B8 spreading out from a source
C2 drying
C5 seismic heat loss
F7 can be internal or partial

G8 splitting
H5 cause of shadow zones in Earth
I1 liquifying
I9 important in electricity and heat

47 OHM'S CODES

Throughout history, scientists have protected the priority of their discoveries in different ways. Galileo for example used anagrams in clearly dated letters to prove that he had made discoveries at certain times. He could thus continue researching a topic without giving his competitors clues so that they could leap-frog his work. Others have used codes to communicate ideas. The codes below represent codes that Georg Ohm may have used, back in 1827.

If the alphabet is reversed (a is z, b is y, c is x etc.) Ohm's law becomes:

Xfiivmg / rh / kilkligrlmzo / gl / klgvmgrzo / wruuvivmxv / uli / z / ivhrhgzmxv / driv / ag / xlmhgzmg / gvnkvizgfiv.

a What is this statement of Ohm's law?

The same law in a different code is:

Dvssfou / jt / qspqpsujpobm / up / qpufoujbm / ejggfsfodf / gps / b / sftjtubodf / xjsf / bu / dpotubou / ufnqfsbuvsf.

b What is the key to the code?

Slightly more difficult, we have, for the same law:

3g18j5n8 / s19 / l18m16m18h9m14a12 / h15 / l15h5n20s1p / 4s6v5j5n3w / 6m18 / a / 18w19s19h1n3w / 23s18w / 1h / 3m14i20a14h / 20w13l5j1h21j5.

c What is the key to the code?

d What is the code for this law when the key is:

"Reverse the alphabet letters and then take the letter after it."

e Who might have made the following code to protect his discovery?

L18w19i21j5 / a14x / 22m12g13w / 15v / 1 / v9d5x / 13a19i / 15v / 7a19 / a20 / y15n19h1n20 / h5o16w18a20g18w / 1j5 / s14f5j19w12c / 16j15l15j20s15n1p.

48 DIFFRACTION LOGIC

The angle (ϴ) of each order (m) by a diffraction grating with spacing (d) is given by the equation $m\lambda = d \sin\theta$.

$m\lambda = d \sin\theta$		m: 1	m: 2	m: 3	m: 4	d /µm: 800	d /µm: 1600	d /µm: 2400	d /µm: 3200	θ° (2sf): 30	θ° (2sf): 39	θ° (2sf): 43	θ° (2sf): 58
λ /nm	450												
	500												
	550												
	600												
θ° (2sf)	30												
	39												
	43												
	58												
d /µm	800												
	1600												
	2400												
	3200												

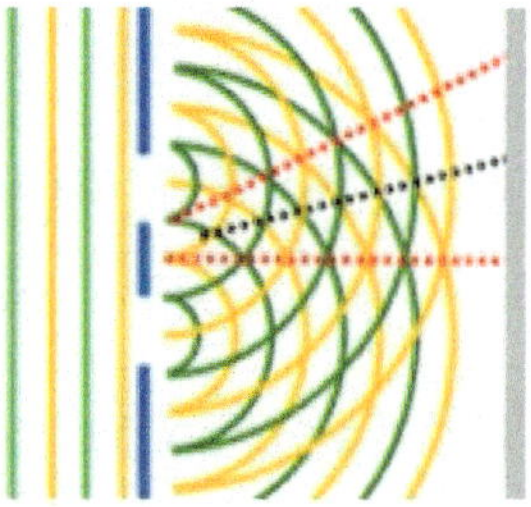

[Note, the angles are the most difficult to measure.]

A When λ = 600 nm, m = 2 and d = 2400 µm, sinϴ = 0.5.

B The slit width for 43˚ was 800 µm and λ was >500 nm.

C The line for the shortest λ was for m = 3 and d = 1600 µm.

D The line for the largest angle was not for d = 3200 µm.

49 CROSSSUMS ELECTRICITY

Complete the crosssums grid by finding the numbers for the clues.

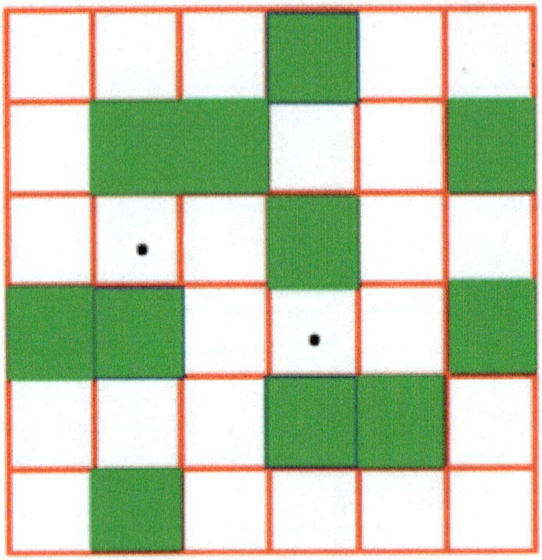

resistance when a p.d. of 36 V produces a current of 10 A

energy in J supplied when a p.d. of 9 V produces a current of 2 A for 5 s

I in a 5 m length of wire when $B = 5 \times 10^{-4}$ T gives $F = 1.7 \times 10^{-2}$ N

in a 100% efficient transformer, N_p when $V_p = 240$ V, $V_s = 12$ V and $N_s = 286$

in a 100% efficient transformer, V_p when $I_s = 0.6$ A, $V_s = 380$ V and $I_p = 3$ A

power when a current of 27 A is driven by a p.d. of 12 V

current in mA when a charge of 4896 C flows in a time of 1000 s

useful output when 528 J of energy is put into a 75% efficient machine

energy given to 0.3326 C of charge falling through a p.d. of 25 000 V

50 CANDLE POWER

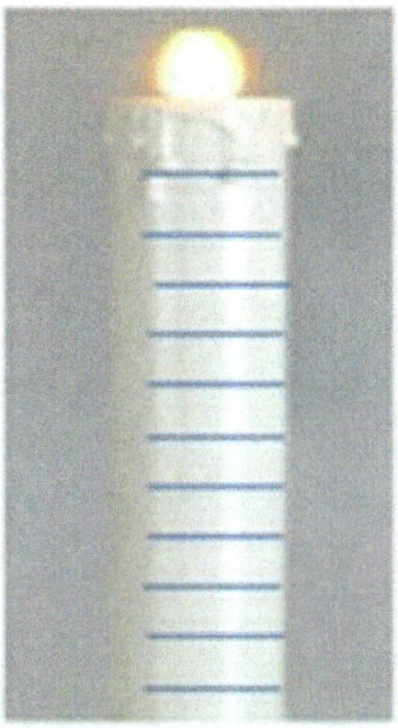

1 Candles have long been used as timers. Equal lengths of a uniform diameter candle take the same time to burn.
So, a uniform candle can be made into a timer by subdividing it into equal parts.
How could you change the candle to measure shorter time intervals? Is there more than one way?

2 **Imagine you only had one uncalibrated candle which you knew took exactly 5 minutes to burn away and a second such candle which burnt away in 8 minutes.**
How could you use these two candles to measure the time to boil an egg for exactly 3 minutes, without measuring lengths.

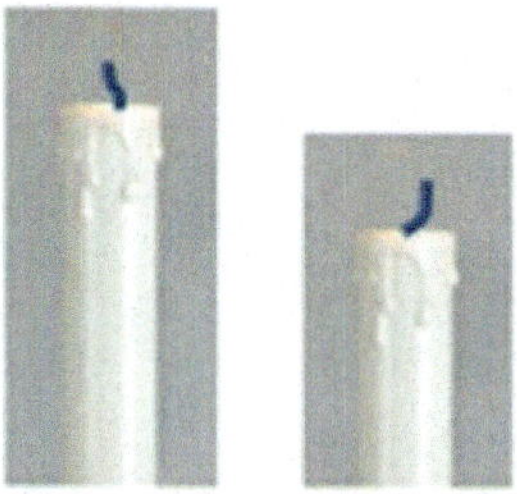

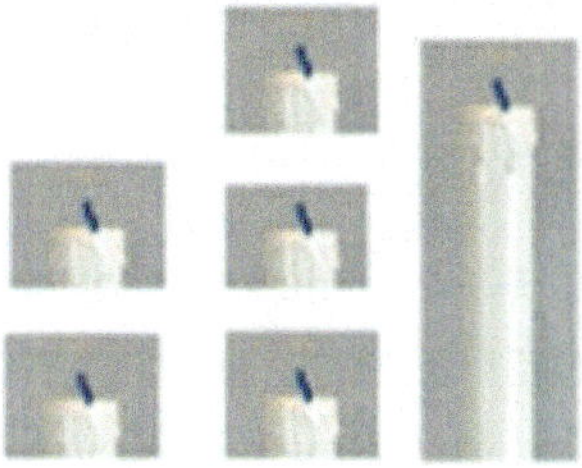

3 The unburnt end of five candles can be joined to produce a full candle. Each full candle burns for exactly 1 hour.

a Starting with 125 full candles, for how long will you be able to get light?

b In practice, there will be one period of enforced darkness. Why is this?

51 HOT AND COLD WORDFIT

Fit the words below into this grid.

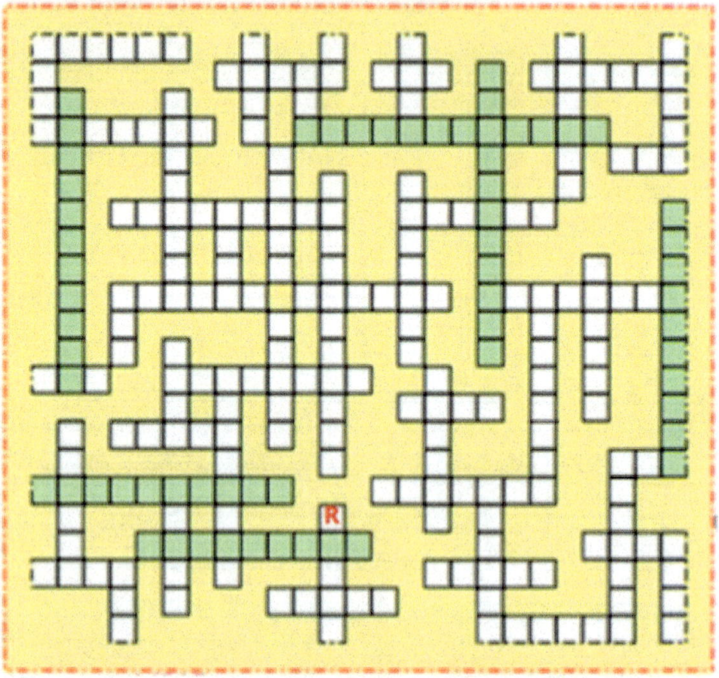
R

12 CONDENSATION

11 EVAPORATION
TEMPERATURE
THIXOTROPIC

10 CONDUCTION
CONVECTION

9 MICROWAVE
RADIATION

8 ABSOLUTE
CAPACITY
FREEZING
INFRARED
SPECIFIC

7 BOILING
CELSIUS
SKATING
THERMAL

6 CAVERN
ENERGY
FROZEN
FRYING
HEATER
IGLOOS
KELVIN
LATENT
LIQUID
SKIING
VAPOUR

5 CRACK
DENSE
FROST
INUIT
PISTE
POLAR
ROAST
SOLID
TOAST

4 COLD
HEAT
OVEN
RAIN
RATE
RINK
SNOW
STEW
WADE
ZERO

3 ARC
FOG
GAS
ICE
SET
SUN
WET

2 AT
OR

For the words fitting in the six shaded rectangles:

1 which process is responsible for many earthquakes?

2 which process produces most energy loss from a cup of tea?

3 which two processes are opposites?

4 what is the meaning of the word beginning with T?

52 QUINTAINES AND LIMERICKS

Writing (even non-rhyming) poems is a great way of exploring a topic. Restricting the number of words / syllables makes you think carefully about each word, to fit a rule. A simple type is the 5-line poem (a quintaine). It may explore things such as an object, a process or an idea.

Guess the intended first or last word of these quintaines:

....

Not inertia

Exploding or colliding

Equal and opposite forces

Conservation

A meter

Electrons flow

To and fro

Timed charge counter

....

There once was a teacher called Joule,

Whose car was exceedingly cool.

He did not drive it too fast,

But, inevitably, at last,

It faltered and ran out of ....

Changing

Continually with

Temperature, brightness, length

And thickness also is affective

Controlling charge flow

....

53 GALILEO'S TIME

The earliest recorded stop-watch was made in 1816. Prior to that time, available means for determining time intervals mainly involved the Sun/Moon, e.g. day/night, seasons and sundials plus of course the human pulse.

(1564-1642) is credited among other things with being the Father of Physics and the scientific method. An important aspect of many of his experiments involved estimation of time intervals.

Suggest a situation where each of these is sufficiently precise to do the job.

54 COGS AGAIN

Imagine you have a set up as in puzzle 8, but the cogs have 12, 8 and 5 teeth.

The number showing through the screen is 1 1 1.

a How many times will the 12 teeth cog have to rotate until the numbers again show as 1 1 1?

b What number appears after 5 turns of the 12 teeth cog?

c Describe the effect of swapping round the 8 and the 5 teeth cogs.

d Can you see any relationship between the number of teeth and the number of turns of each cog, for the same number to appear with this arrangement?

e Does your relationship work with the 20, 16 and 12 teeth arrangement of puzzle 8?

55 MORE DINGBATS

15 14 13 12 11 10 9 8 7 6 5 4 3 2 1
e
Flamingo's

VCOULRTRAEGNET

DUCIONT

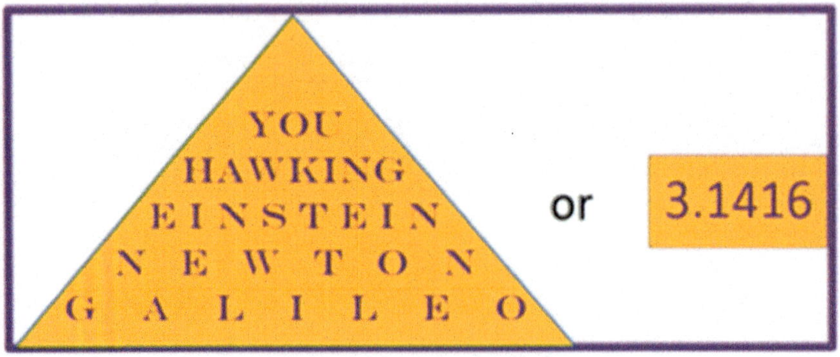
YOU
HAWKING
EINSTEIN
NEWTON
GALILEO
or
3.1416

56 QUARKS AND MESONS

Puzzle 45 showed some rules about quarks in Physics, just as in games.

Now, here is an extra rule in the "Game of quarks":

Protons and neutrons each have a corresponding antiparticle: an antiproton and an antineutron – with charges opposite to the normal particle. They are made from antiquarks, $\bar{u}$ or antiup and $\bar{d}$ or antidown.

a Predict the quark arrangement of an antiproton and an antineutron.

Here is an extension to the rules showing more possibilities:

- **A 'meson' is a type of particle containing one quark and one antiquark.**

Four arrangements of u, d, $\bar{u}$ and $\bar{d}$ are possible.

b Draw a table to show the charges for each arrangement.

And finally (for now!):

- **During beta-minus decay, a neutron becomes a proton.**

i What are the changes in quark arrangement during beta decay?

ii Predict what happens during positron emission.

[You may be interested that physicists have discovered more quarks to play with! They have names like '*strange*', '*charm*', '*top*' and '*bottom/beauty*' quarks.]

[Just as a scrabble activity, can you use the rules of Scrabble to fit the word GRAVITY into the grid of Puzzle 36?]

57 TSUNAMIS AND YOU

Some puzzles have no single correct answer or even no complete, universally accepted answer at all. Such puzzles often involve human interaction with each other or with the natural universe or both.

Tsunamis are naturally occurring events often causing many casualties and untold damage. How do the Aid organisations distribute the large amounts of money they collect, to help people in affected countries?

Imagine that one developing country has received money from a charity to help cope with Tsunamis. How would you advise the government of that country to spend the money.The amount of money available is £50 million.

You read in a book:

Give a hungry person a fish and you provide food for a day. Teach that person to fish and you offer the potential for that individual to obtain food for a life-time and / or to teach many others.

or

Consultation with interested groups raise issues in three categories:

- **immediate aid**
- **rebuilding to replace**
- **preparing for the future!**

Several groups of people suggest how to use some of that money if it was made available. Their suggestions are on the next page.

Photo by Jeffrey Eisen on Unsplash

Tsunamis (cont.)

A. supply people with clean water, food, medicine and tents. Immediate cost £25 million (£25M).
B. increase the rate of hospital construction. Estimated cost £15 M.
C. provide construction materials for homes. Expected outgoings £20 M.
D. strengthen buildings, roads and bridges. Expense likely to be £40 M.
E. improve escape routes and road signs. Anticipated need £5 M.
F. provide early-warning of seismic events. Estimated outlay £10 M.
G. find ways of mitigating tsunami's effects. Forecast rate £3 M per year.
H. erect buildings for emergency relief supplies. Predicted cost £5 M immediately and £3 M per year.

Not all of these requests can be satisfied from the £50M.

a Choose your order of priority for distributing the money.

b Put forward some arguments in favour of the suggestion that you think is most important.

c Can you give any advice to improve the suggestion which you think is least important so that it might attract more money?

ANSWERS

1 WAVE LOGIC

Wave	f (Hz)	v (m/s)
A	10 000	10
B	1 000	1 000
C	100 000	100

2 SOME HISTORY OF SCIENCE

Name	date	contribution to humanity through physics
Archimedes	250BC	explained flotation
Bardeen	1947	invented the transistor
Berners-Lee	1989	invented the internet
Chadwick	1932	discovered neutron
Einstein	1905	discovered the law for the photoelectric effect
Galileo	1610	showed phases of Venus
Hawking	1973	explained the radiation emitted from black holes
Newton	1687	formulated the law of universal gravitation
Rutherford	1911	discovered the nucleus
Thomson	1897	discovered electron

3 MOTION CROSSLINES

PLANE
VECTOR
DISTANCE
SPEED
ALPHA
GRADIENT
FORCE
SCALAR
INERTIA
CENTRIPETAL
STATIONARY
UNIFORM

4 ASTRONOMY CROSSWORD

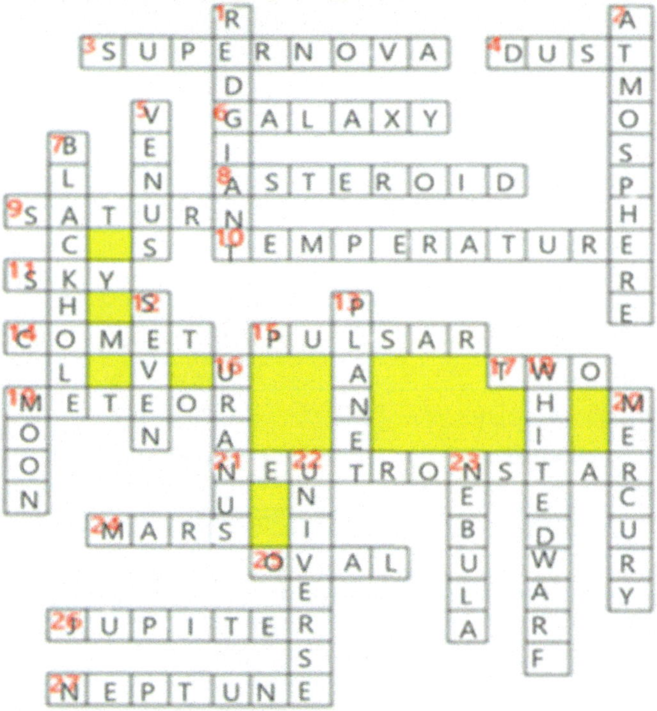
REDGIANT
ATMOSPHERE
SUPERNOVA
DUST
VENUS
GALAXY
BLACKHOLE
ASTEROID
SATURN
TEMPERATURE
SKY
SEVEN
PLANE
COMET
PULSAR
URANUS
TWO
WHITEDWARF
METEOR
MOON
MERCURY
NEUTRONSTAR
UNIVERSE
NEBULA
MARS
OVAL
JUPITER
NEPTUNE

5 ANAGRAMS OF FAMOUS PHYSICISTS

AMPERE	ARCHIMEDES	CELSIUS
COPERNICUS	CURIE	EINSTEIN
FAHRENHEIT	FARADAY	FLEMING
GALILEO	GALVANI	GAUSS
GEIGER	ISAAC NEWTON	RUTHERFORD

6 CROSSSUMS

■	2	2	.	0
2	■	2	■	■
0	.	0	2	2
2	■	2	■	2
0	.	2	2	2

a row 3

b 22022, 2020, 222, 22.0, 0.222, 0.022

c 22022, (2020, 222 and 0.222 and 22.0), 0.022

7 PHYSCS DS WTHT VWLS 1

Density is mass/volume.

Pressure equals force over area.

Force is proportional to extension.

Power is the rate of doing work.

Force equals mass times acceleration.

Momentum is mass times velocity.

Angle of incidence equals angle of reflection.

Acceleration equals the rate of change of velocity.

Wave speed equals frequency times wavelength.

Weight equals mass times gravitational field strength.

The speed of a satellite can be constant but the velocity changes

Red shift of galaxies provides evidence that the Universe is expanding.

All electromagnetic waves are transverse and travel at the same speed in a vacuum

8 COG PICTURE

a 12 times b 10 times

9 IT TAKES 2 CROSSWORD

NEWTON
ACTION
THRUST
UPTHRUST
ARCHIMEDES
ACCELERATION
KINETIC
FULCRUM
MOMENTUM
RESULTANT
LIFT
HORIZONTAL
POTENTIAL
BALANCED
REACTION
INERTIA
TERMINAL
SPEED
PIVOT
TORQUE
DRAG
GRAVITY
CLOCKWISE

10 RAINBOW

The correct order of answers to fit the grid is:

prism spread yellow refraction violet orange blue magenta

and the word in the shaded vertical rectangle is SPECTRUM.

11 DINGBATS 1

'average speed' 'infrared' [put 'red' in 'fra']

12 MORE DINGBATS

variable resistor **radioactive decay** **refractive index**

13 GOING ROUND THE MOON(S)

a **90° in both cases**

b

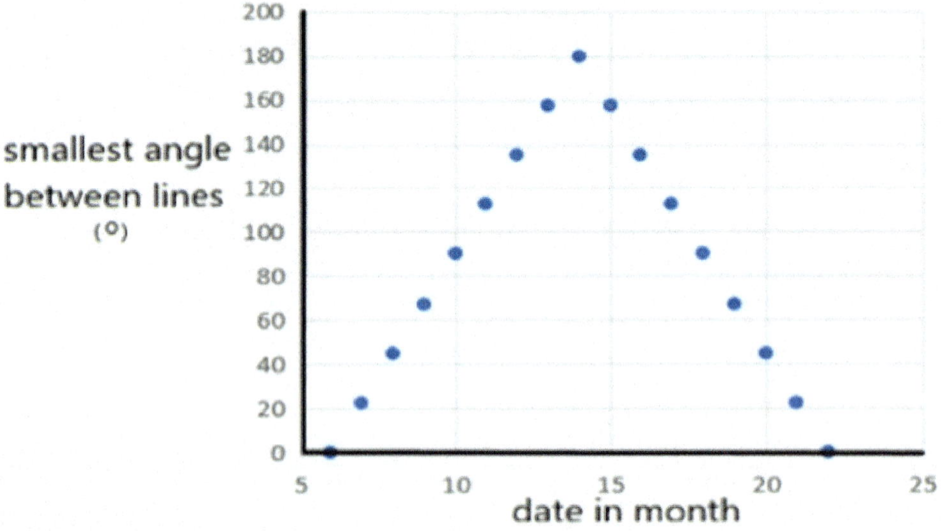
smallest angle
between lines
(°)
200
180
160
140
120
100
80
60
40
20
0
5
10
15
20
25
date in month

14 DENSE LOGIC

	mass / kg	volume / m^3	density/kg/m^3
K	0.64	8.0×10^{-4}	800
L	5.44	4.0×10^{-4}	13600
M	1.40	5.0×10^{-4}	2800
N	2.10	2.0×10^{-4}	10500

15 MEASURING VOLUME

ai 1l Fill 4l glass.

Pour water from 4l into the 3l to completely fill the 3l glass.

Exactly 1l remains in the 4l glass.

2l You could, at a trivial level,

Obtain 1l as above and put that into the bowl.

Repeat above to obtain 2l.

OR (slightly more interestingly)

Fill the 3l and pour into 4l.

Refill the 3l and top up the 4l - 2l now remains in the 3l glass.

ii At a trivial level, you could obtain 1l seven times to add to the bowl.

We could write this in shorthand as: (7x1=7)

OR (3+4=7) OR (1+3+3=7) OR (3x5 – 4x2 = 7) Ad infinitum (and beyond?)!!!

OR

Pour four lots of 4l into the bowl. Use 3l to remove three complete glasses from bowl. (4x4 – 3x3=7)

b Here are some examples:

	(3l and 5l)	(4l and 7l)
1	3 into 5, a second 3 into 5 leaves 1 in 3	4 into 7, a second 4 into 7 leaves 1 in 4
2	5 into 3 leaves 2 in 5	2x 7 in bowl and remove 4x3 leaves 2 in bowl
3		7 into 4 leaves 3 in 7
4	2 x (5 into 3 leaves 2 in 5)	
5		4x3 into bowl and remove 7x1
6	3x2	(7 into 4 leaves 3 – put in bowl) twice
7	5x2 into bowl and remove 3x1	
8	5 into 3 and put rest of 5 in to bowl - four times	4x2
9	3x3	4x4 – 7
10	5x2	7x2into bowl and – 4x1

16 EARTHQUAKE CROSSWORD

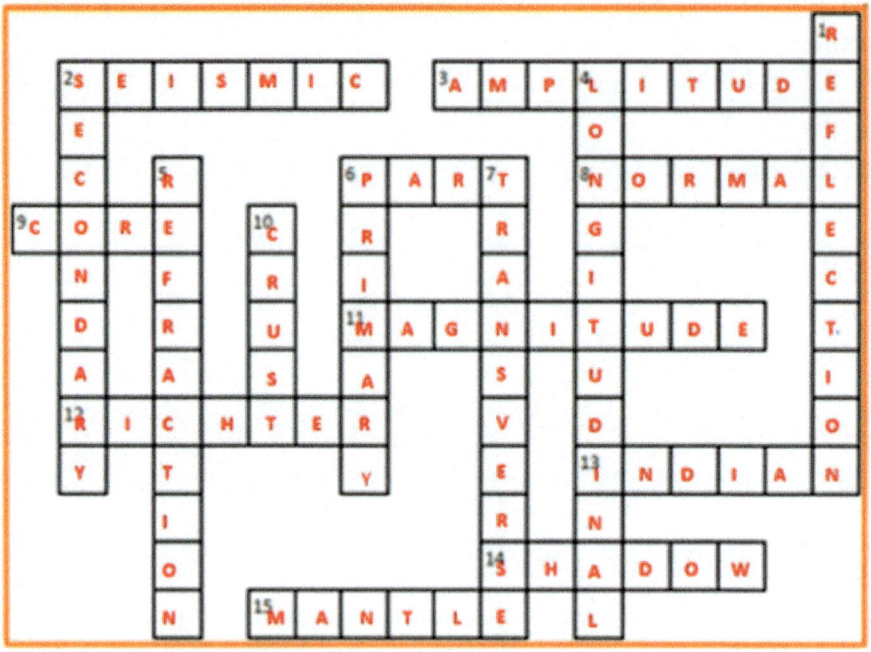
1 REFLECTION
2 SEISMIC
SECONDARY
3 AMPLITUDE
4 LONGITUDINAL
5 REFRACTION
6 PART
PRIMARY
7 TRANSVERSE
8 NORMAL
9 CORE
10 CRUST
11 MAGNITUDE
12 RICHTER
13 INDIAN
14 SHADOW
15 MANTLE

17 UNITS WORDFIT

VOLT
OHM
BECQUEREL
MOLE
LUMEN
KILOGRAM
MHO
CURIE
JOULE
PARSEC
METRE
REM
COULOMB
CANDELA
BARN
NEWTON
KELVIN
AMPERE
SECOND
DAY
HOUR
WATT

18 ILLUMINATING WRITING

a Galileo made tremendously important discoveries in astronomy not just looking at the stars but also observing 4 moons orbiting Jupiter which led to the heliocentric view of the Solar System. Here the telescope replaces one 'l' observing the star on the 'i'and the Jovian 'o' being accompanied by an appropriate number of acolytes.

b Newton is noted, possibly apocryphally, for discovering gravity due to an apple falling from a malus tree.

At the centre of Joule's work is the energy shown here written in the form of the 'u'.

The electrical symbol for 'earth' is shown here as the letter E which it resembles in some ways.

The word 'transformer' is spelt out as a set of downwards steps. So it is going further than just the simple word to include the idea of 'step-down'.

19 CLUEDOKU RADIOACTIVITY

A7;2 C2;1 D8;4 E5;9 F2;3 G3;7 G4;5 H7;6 I6;8

4	**2**	3	**7**	6	**1**	8	**5**	**9**
7	**9**	1	8	**5**	3	4	**2**	**6**
8	**5**	6	**9**	2	**4**	7	**1**	**3**
9	**1**	**2**	**6**	7	**8**	5	3	**4**
3	**4**	**8**	1	9	5	6	**7**	**2**
5	6	**7**	**3**	**4**	**2**	**1**	9	8
2	8	**4**	**5**	**3**	**7**	**9**	6	**1**
6	**3**	5	4	1	9	**2**	**8**	**7**
1	7	9	**2**	8	**6**	**3**	**4**	**5**

20 EARTHQUAKE LOGIC

earthquake	year	magnitude	deaths
Kashmir	2005	7.6	86 700
Myanmar	1988	7.3	3
Nepal	1934	8.0	8 000
Sumatra	2004	9.2	250 000

21 DINGBATS 2

Mexican wave **angle of refraction** **alternating current**

ice cube **upthrust**

22 MORE DINGBATS 2

IN CAN DESCENT

m/s

RESULTANT FORCE

ACCELERATION DUE TO GRAVITY

23 WAYS TO 'WEIGH'

a The official mass of a newly minted coin is 3.56 g. Mass decreases with use but may increase due to grease and dust.

Your value will be good if you get between 2.5 and 4.5g.

b The exact size/squareness of the weight holder does not matter – it will be balanced against a variable amount of piece of modelling clay. More care is needed to ensure the 'weights' are equal as they must be as equal as possible.

24 BALANCING WEIGHTS

a A > C and C > B so also A > B

b P = 18 and R = 15

25 VIEWING BABIES

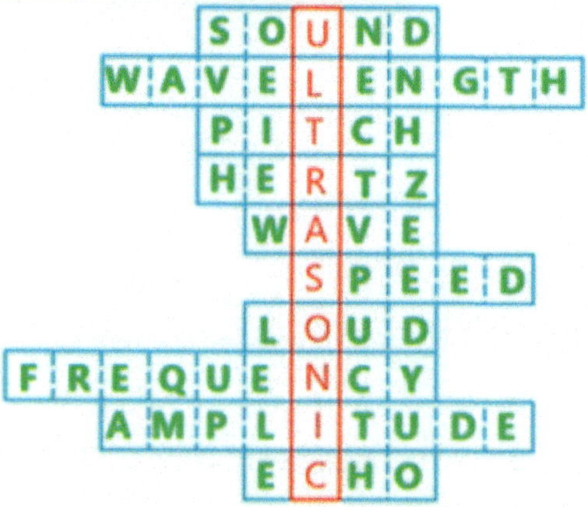
SOUND
WAVELENGTH
PITCH
HERTZ
WAVE
SPEED
LOUD
FREQUENCY
AMPLITUDE
ECHO

26 FORCE AND MOTION WORD SEARCH

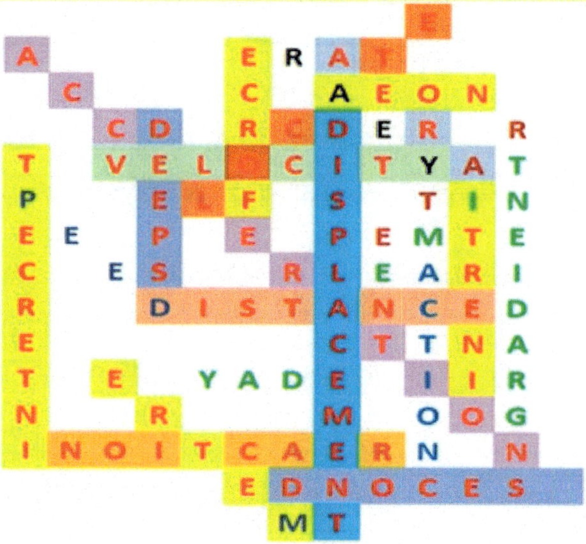

27 FEELING HOT?

a 32°F and 212°F

bi an estimate (ball-park figure) would be somewhere between 125 and 155°F bii 140°F biii 99°F

28 OR HOTTER?

a At home, it is a lot more attractive than most thermometers and, due to the way it operates, may be a more entertaining prospect than watching grass grow or wallpaper drying.

b The precision needed is very difficult to achieve – my thermometer (as pictured) indicates temperatures to the nearest 2°C. In addition, a large amount of heat is needed to change the temperature of the large amount if fluid it contains. This would seriously affect the temperature of its surroundings thus changing the conditions of the experiment.

c The changes in body temperature recorded in hospitals would be virtually impossible to measure and would take a very long time to show. The size of the thermometer would be quite uncomfortable for the patient!

29 RADIOACTIVITY CROSSWORD

CONTAMINATION
ELECTROSTATIC
TOMOGRAPHY
THERMAL
NEUTRONS
CHARGE
FUSION
BECQUEREL
ISOTOPES
PROTON
FISSION
CANCER
BACKGROUND
SCARF
MUTATION
ALPHA
DECREASES
HALFLIFE
GAMMA
ELECTRON
CURIE
RANDOM
MASS
NUCLEUS
POSITRON
ION

30 THERMAL LOGIC

OBJECT	MASS / kg	SHC /J/kg/˚C	TEMP. CHANGE/ ˚C
W	2	2100	40
X	4	1800	60
Y	1	2000	80
Z	3	4200	20

31 DINGBATS 3

radioactive half-life step-up transformer hindsight infrasound

32 RADIOACTIVE LOGIC

material	energy of beam/units	charge number	mass number
A	10	+1	1
B	15	-1	small
C	20	0	0
D	5	+2	4

33 PHYSCS DS WTHT VWLS (2)

Stress is proportional to strain.

Like poles repel, unlike poles attract.

Force equals rate of change of momentum.

Energy transferred equals charge x potential difference.

Half-life is the time taken for half the undecayed nuclei to decay.

Work done equals force multiplied by distance moved in the direction of the force.

Waves transfer energy and information without transferring matter.

Change in thermal energy can be calculated from mass x specific heat capacity x change in temperature.

For a body to be at constant temperature it needs to radiate the same average power that it absorbs.

Fission of uranium 235 produces two daughter nuclei and two or more neutrons plus release of energy.

Energy cannot be created or destroyed merely changed from one form to another.

34 ELECTROMAGNETIC WAVE

C	O	M	M	U	N	I	C	A	T	E
		D	I	S	H					
	R	E	C	E	I	V	E	R		
I	N	F	R	A	R	E	D			
		M	O	B	I	L	E			
			W	A	T	E	R			
		R	A	D	I	O				
		O	V	E	N					
A	N	T	E	N	N	A				

35 PHYSICS ANAGRAMS

In alphabetical order:

acceleration amplitude displacement frequencies inertia magnets momentum neutrons particle proton radioactivity resistance temperatures thermistor transformer transistor wavelength

action and reaction are equal and opposite

36 ELECTRIC CROSSFIT

37 COUNTING ROUND THE BEND

a **64 and 16**

b **change direction of arrow 6**

38 MAKING A 'CUPPA' TEA

You begin by inverting both simultaneously.

a 8 = Start timing on first inversion, then invert again when 5 finishes. 8 is when 3 finishes.

6 = Start timing by inverting until 3 ends then invert until 3 ends.

2 = Start timing when 3 finishes. 2 is when 5 finishes now. (5 – 3)

1 = Let 3 finish. Invert 3 only. Start timing when 5 finishes and stop when 3 now finishes.

b Begin by inverting both simultaneously.

1 = Start timing when 3 finshes and finish timing when 4 finishes.

2 = When 3 finishes, invert it as fast as possible. Start timing when 4 finishes and stop timing when 3 finishes again.

5 = As 1 but then invert 4 as fast as possible.

c 2 = invert 4 and then 5 when they each finish. Start timing when 4 ends the second time and stop when 5 ends the second time.

3 = as 2 but three inversions each OR invert 4 twice but start timing when 5 finishes and stop when 4 ends the second time.

7 = Start timing when 5 finishes but invert 4 quickly as soon as it finishes twice. Finish timing as 4 finishes the third time

d 3.3×10^{-24}s

39 CLUEDOKU RADIOACTIVITY

1	4	8	3	7	6	9	5	2
3	7	2	5	9	1	4	8	6
5	9	6	4	8	2	1	3	7
6	1	9	7	3	5	8	2	4
8	2	3	6	1	4	7	9	5
7	5	4	9	2	8	6	1	3
9	3	5	1	4	7	2	6	8
2	6	7	8	5	9	3	4	1
4	8	1	2	6	3	5	7	9

40 FAMOUS PHYSICISTS CROSSWORD

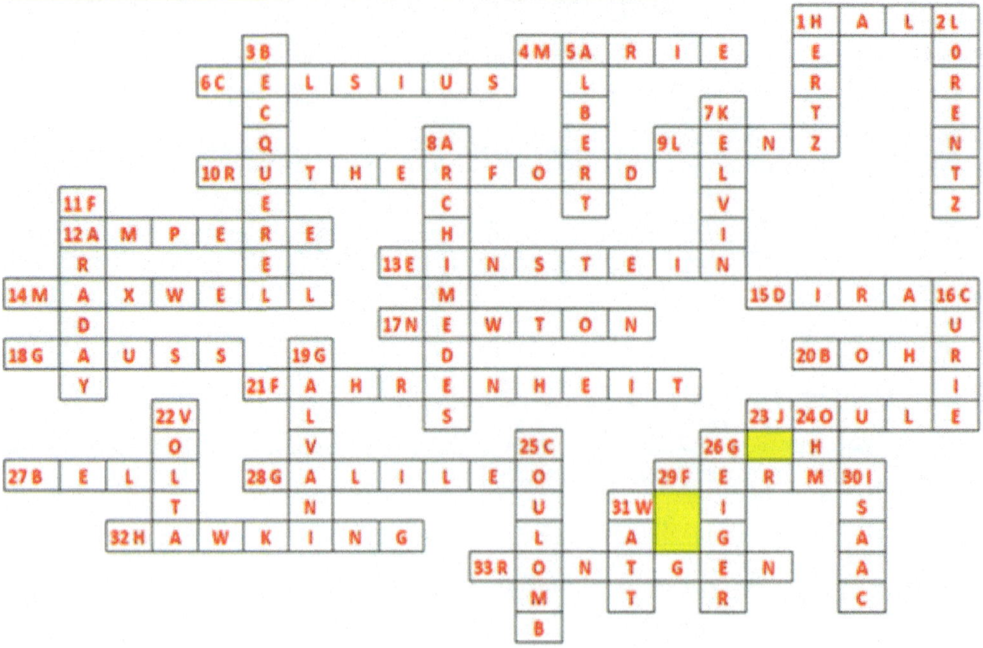
1 HALL
1 HERTZ
2 LORENTZ
3 BECQUEREL
4 MARIE
5 ALBERT
6 CELSIUS
7 KELVIN
8 ARCHIMEDES
9 LENZ
10 RUTHERFORD
11 FARADAY
12 AMPERE
13 EINSTEIN
14 MAXWELL
15 DIRAC
16 CURIE
17 NEWTON
18 GAUSS
19 GALVANI
20 BOHR
21 FAHRENHEIT
22 VOLTA
23 JOULE
24 OHM
25 COULOMB
26 GEIGER
27 BELL
28 GALILEO
29 FERMI
30 ISAAC
31 WATT
32 HAWKING
33 RONTGEN

41 BODE'S WELL FOR PLANETS

a

planet	predicted orbital radius / units	actual orbital radius / units
MERCURY	0.4	0.39
VENUS	0.7	0.72
Earth	1	1
Mars	1.6	1.52
Jupiter	2.8	5.20
SATURN	5.2	9.60
URANUS	10.0	19.2
Neptune	19.6	30.0

b All four predictions lie within about 5% of the actual value. This is good agreement.

c Jupiter, Saturn and Uranus are about 54% -52% different, while Neptune is over 65% out. They do not fit the pattern.

d Certainly helps! You may have noticed that the actual value for Jupiter is the same as the predicted value for Saturn. This would be in perfect agreement then if Jupiter became the fifth planet out rather than the fourth. Saturn, Uranus and Neptune would also fit the pattern well if moved one planet further away.

e If Neptune was not a natural part of the Solar System, then Pluto would be the 8th planet. Its predicted value would then be 38.8 units while the actual mean value for Pluto is 39.5 – agreeing within 2%. Other factors support this quite strong evidence for Neptune having been captured by the Sun's gravity to occupy a planetary position.

42 GUESSING OR ESTIMATING

a

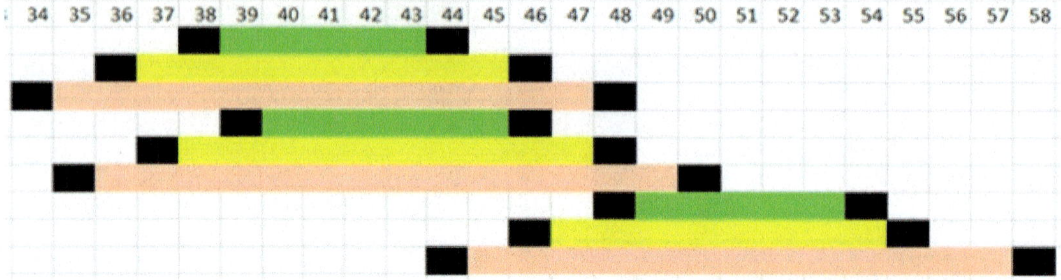
34 35 36 37 38 39 40 41 42 43 44 45 46 47 48 49 50 51 52 53 54 55 56 57 58

The maximum range for the number is 34 (41 – 7) to 58 (51 + 7).
The black squares show the values for each difference from each guess.
The current value must have three black squares (46 or 48) with one of each colour – **48**.

b

41 42 43 44 45 46 47 48 49 50 51 52 53 54 55 56 57 58 59 60 61 62 63 64 65 66 67 68 69

The trees are **47 m** apart. Here, there is only one number with three black squares.

Both of these involve estimates since there is a comparison either against the brightness of a bulb for a known current or against the tree separation against the height of woodsmen ie about 2 m.

43 CURRENT AFFAIRS

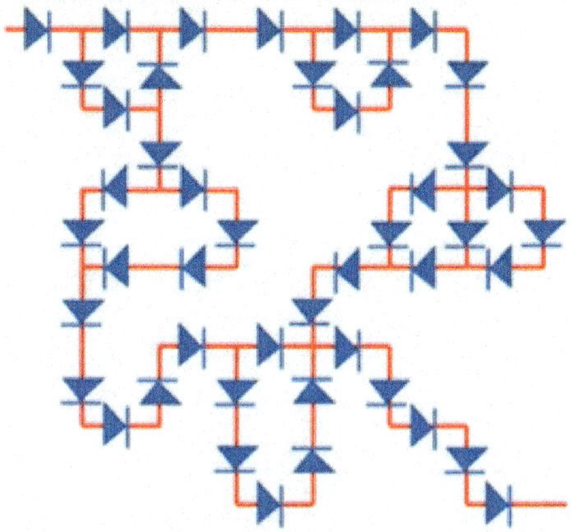

OR

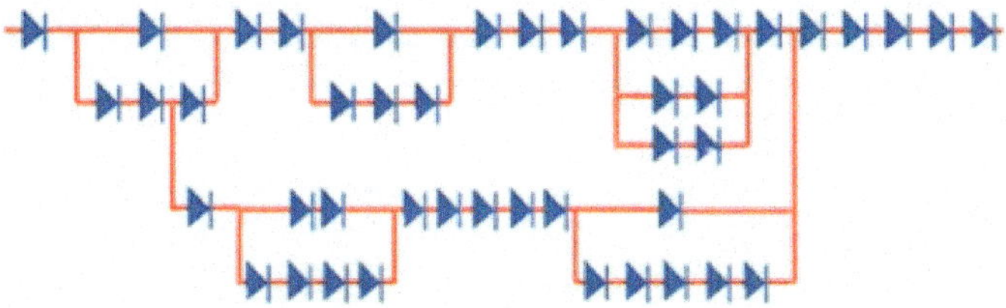

44 ESTIMATING / MEASURING

a 6.3×10^{-4} ly

b 2.7×10^{5} **AU**

c 1 apc is approximately the same as 3.1 cm which is approximatelyn the same as the average length of a thumb.

di the size of a persons's hand differs according to age, gender, height, mass etc.

ii about (!) 1.9×10^{24}

45 RULES OF THE GAME – QUARKS

a 20 b zebra (with z on the double-letter score c 5x1 +4x3

d Use the R of scrabble and this also uses two double word squares

e Using the e already present scores 20, using the two triple-letter squares

f RABBLE has already used the two B's in the set and so it is impossible for the next person to choose one.

g RULES: 3 quarks in each but of only 2 types so some possibilities are that:

- one type of quark has a charge of +1 (equal in size to the charge on an electron but positive) and the other type is uncharged. Here, the proton has 2 charged and 1 uncharged and a neutron all 3 uncharged.
- one type is uncharged and the other has a charge of $+\frac{1}{2}$ so a proton is 2 charged and 1 uncharged while a neutron has all 3 uncharged.
- one type is uncharged and the other has a charge of $+\frac{1}{3}$ so a proton has 3 charged and the neutron has all 3 uncharged.
- although it may seem like a trick(!), the values scientists are presently working with are shown in this table:

quark	charge
Up / u	$+\frac{2}{3}$ electronic charge
Down / d	$-\frac{1}{3}$ electronic charge

So, how do these follow the rules to form protons and neutrons? The answer is upside down here.

	number of up	number of down
proton	2	1
neutron	1	2

46 CLUEDOKU PROCESSES

9	8	7	5	6	3	4	2	1
1	2	4	9	8	7	3	5	6
6	3	5	1	4	2	9	7	8
5	9	1	3	7	6	2	8	4
2	6	3	8	1	4	7	9	5
7	4	8	2	9	5	1	6	3
3	5	9	4	2	8	6	1	7
8	7	2	6	3	1	5	4	9
4	1	6	7	5	9	8	3	2

47 OHM'S CODES

a Current is proportional to potential difference for a resistance wire at constant temperature.

b Take the next letter in the alphabet.

c a for z and letter after, alternated with number for letter

d Ygjjwnh si ljmlmjhsmnap hm lmhwnhsap xsvvwjwnyw vmj a jwisihanyw esjw ah ymnihanh hwolwjahgjw.

e This is Boyle's law for gases:
Pressure and volume of a fixed mass of gas, at constant temperature, are inversely proportional.

48 DIFFRACTION LOGIC

m	λ	d	θ
1	550	800	43
2	600	2400	30
3	450	1600	58
4	500	3200	39

49 CROSSSUMS ELECTRICITY

3	2	4		4	5
9			3	8	
6	•	8		9	0
		3	•	6	
7	9	1			1
6		5	7	2	0

50 CANDLE POWER

1 **You could make the markings closer together or alternatively you could probably make the candle of smaller diameter.**

2 **Start both candles burning at the same time and put the egg in boiling water when the 5 minute candle goes out. The egg will be ready when the 8 minute candle goes out.**

3a **156 (125 + 25 + 5 +1) hours**

3b **While waiting after the last unburnt end is produced ready to make the last full candle.**

51 HOT AND COLD WORDFIT

1 Convection 2 Evaporation

3 Evaporation and condensation relate to the movement of particles through the liquid/vapour boundary. In evaporation, the particles go from liquid to gas while the opposite happens during condensation.

4 Some materials, like ketchup, have high viscosity when still but flow easily when shaken. Such materials are described as thixotropic.

52 QUINTAINS AND LIMERICKS

a momentum b ammeter c fuel d variable resistor

53 GALILEO'S TIME

heart beat (pulse) is used in medical diagnosis as a quick, non-invasive way of indicating whether the heart is working at a normal rate. Too high / too low a rate indicates something may be wrong.

A chandelier was reputed to have been used by Galileo when investigating motion with candleholders swinging from a high roof in a cathedral.

Sundials are sufficiently precise to tell you when it is about time for lunch or dinner if you are working outdoors. Unfortunately you might go hungry in rainy days or in the winter.

Egg timers are particularly useful when a fixed time is required, such as when brewing tea or boiling an egg.

Candles have been used for millenia for the light they produce and also as indicators of time. They might be particularly useful as indicators of when parties should break up if there was no electricity.

Stopwatches can be quite precise but also can be stopped and restarted easily during sportive / scientific situations.

54 COGS AGAIN

a 10 times **b** 131 **c** each of the 8 and 5 teeth cogs will show the same number but will rotate in opposite direction to before **d** the number of teeth on a cog x the number of rotations is equal for all three cogs (120 here) **e** yes, but the common number is 240 in that case.

55 MORE DINGBATS

Fleming's left hand rule

Alternating voltage and current

in duct ion

5 significant figures

56 QUARKS AND MESONS

a

quark combination	charge
$u\,\bar{d}$	+1
$u\,\bar{u}$	0
$\bar{u}\,d$	-1
$d\,\bar{d}$	0

bi Neutron (udd) becomes proton (uud) so one d has changed to a u.

bii Proton (uud) becomes neutron (udd) so one u has changed to a d.

Scrabble activity: G is at 11 across 6 down, and the word is vertical.

57 TSUNAMI AND YOU

Some puzzles have no single correct answer or even no complete answer at all. Such puzzles often involve human interaction with others or with nature or with both.

Photo by John Middlekoop on Unsplash

Photo by Sunyu Kim - Unsplash

Please supply your own suggested answers to this Tsunami puzzle.

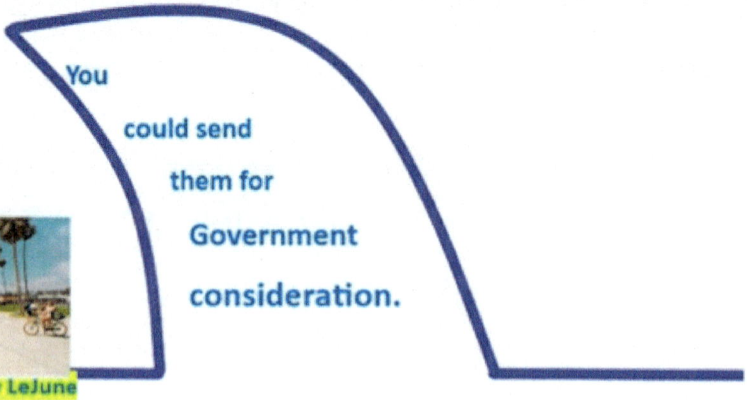
You
could send
them for
Government
consideration.

Photo by Matthew LeJune on Unsplash

Printed in Great Britain
by Amazon

78326739R00052